Read The Bible In 90 Days

Mary Favors

Daily Devotion
Journal
Study Guide
(For Group and Personal)

Divine Favors Christian Publication

ISBN: 1-4243-1-1320-1

Published by:
Divine Favors Christian
Books & Publication
1811 Hwy. 138 SW
Riverdale, GA 30296

Or
P.O Box 44722
Atlanta, GA 30336
404-453-0601

Printed in the United States of America

To order online, please visit our website:
www.divinefavors.com

Dedication

This book is dedicated to God our Heavenly Father, our Lord and Savior Jesus Christ; and the Holy Spirit. Father God I thank you for your love and for sending your Son Jesus. Lord Jesus I thank You; for your obedience and love for the Father. I thank you for shedding your blood and dying on the cross for my sins and the world sins. Thank You Heavenly Father for sending your Holy Spirit; and thank You Holy Spirit for Coming. Thank You for your Guidance and living within me and upon me.

Appreciation

I praise and thank God for my husband Bobby L. Favors. I appreciation your love and your support in all I do. I love you and grateful to the Lord for joining and keeping us together.

To my son Bobby Ja'rrell Favors I thank God for giving us you. Thank you for your support and love. I know you will become all God called you to be.

Receive Your New Life In Christ Jesus

Read Scriptures before praying.

For all have sinned, and come short of the glory of God: (Rom.3:2 3)

Being justified freely by his grace through the redemption that is in Christ Jesus. (Rom.3: 24)

For God so loved the world; that He gave His only begotten Son, that whosoever believeth in Him should not perish, but have everlasting Life. (John 3:16)

For God sent not His Son into the world to condemn the world; But; that the world through Him might be saved. (John 3:17)

He that believeth on Him is not condemned: but he that believeth not is condemned already, because he hath not believed in the name of the only begotten Son of God. (John 3:18)

But God commend His love toward us, in that, while we were yet sinners, Christ died for us. (Rom.5:8)

Let this mind be in you, which was also in Christ Jesus: Who, being in the form of God, thought it not robbery to be equal with God:

But made Himself of no reputation, and took upon Him the form of a servant, and was made in the likeness of men: And being found in fashion as a man, He humbles Himself, and became obedient unto that if thou shalt confess with thy mouth the Lord Jesus, and shalt believe in thine heart that God hath raised Him from the dead, thou shalt be saved. For with the heart man believeth unto righteousness; and with the mouth confession is made unto salvation. For whosoever shall call upon the name of the Lord shall be saved. (Rom.10: 9, 10, 13)

The Prayer of Salvation

Dear God my Heavenly Father, I come to you in the name of Jesus. I know I am a sinner and ask you to forgive me of all my sins. I believe Jesus Christ is Your Son; and He shed His blood and died on the cross for my sins. Jesus went to hell and defeated Satan; on the third day God raised Him from the dead; and is now at the right hand of God praying for me to over come the evil of this world that I might have life and have it more Abundantly. I ask You, Lord Jesus to come into my heart and my life; I need Your help to live this life. I cannot live this life in true victory without You. I pray that You fill me with your Holy Spirit; that you sent in your place Lord Jesus. You said the Holy Spirit will comfort, teach, guide me into the ways of the Father so that I can become one with You. Thank You Holy Spirit for living within and upon me right now in the name of Jesus.

Thank You Lord for my salvation.

Welcome to the Family

Now you need a church home.

I pray and you pray that the Holy Spirit will guide and led you to a church where God's Word is being lived and taught.

In The Name Of Jesus

Preface

Here is an easy-to-read and understanding guide on how to read the Bible in 90 days. This unique guide will begin a life long habit of "Fellowship and Personal Intimate time with the Lord". Revelation 1:3, blessed is he that readeth and they that hear the words.

The Bible is God's revelation to man. It is the only book that gives us accurate information about God, man's need and God's provision for that need.

We all benefit when we read the Bible on a daily basis - regardless of how much or how little time we set aside to read God's Word. This Guide is to help, just because you desire to spend more time with God.

You will get daily reading from the Old Testament, New Testament, Psalms and Proverbs. As you feed on the Word of God; He will increase in your life and you will decrease (1Cor. 3:6). Feed your spirit daily just as you feed your body. As your soul prosper you will prosper. (3 John 2)
" Read the Bible in 90 Days" guide can be used with any Bible: The King James Version, The Amplified Bible, The New Living Translation, The New King James, New International Version, New American Standard , and your Bible.

I pray you will be blessed as you read the Bible in 90 days.

Books of the Bible

Old Testament	Abbreviations
Genesis	Gen.
Exodus	Ex.
Leviticus	Lev.
Numbers	Num.
Deuteronomy	Deut.
Joshua	Josh.
Judges	Judg.
Ruth	Ruth
1Samuel	1 Sam.
2 Samuel	2 Sam.
1 Kings	1 Kin.
2King	2 Kin.
1 Chronicles	1 Chr.
2 Chronicles	2 Chr.
Ezra	Ezra
Nehemiah	Neh.
Esther	Esth.
Job	Job
Psalms	Ps.
Proverbs	Prov.
Ecclesiastes	Eccl.
Song of Solomon	Song
Isaiah	Isa.
Jeremiah	Jer.
Lamentations	Lam.
Ezekiel	Ezek.
Daniel	Dan.
Hosea	Hos.
Joel	Joel
Amos	Amos
Obadiah	Obad.

Books of the Bible

Old Testament	Abbreviations
Jonah	Jon.
Micah	Mic.
Nahum	Nah.
Habakkuk	Hab.
Zephaniah	Zeph.
Haggai	Hag.
Zechariah	Zech.
Malachi	Mal.

New Testament	Abbreviations
Matthew	Matt.
Mark	Mark
Luke	Luke
John	John
The Acts	Acts
Romans	Rom.
1 Corinthians	1 Cor.
2 Corinthians	2 Cor.
Galatians	Gal.
Ephesians	Eph.
Philippians	Phil.
Colossians	Col.
1 Thessalonians	1Thess.
2 Thessalonians	2Thess.
1 Timothy	1Tim.
2 Timothy	2Tim.
Titus	Titus
Philemon	Philem..
Hebrews	Heb.
James	James

1 Peter	1 Pet.
2 Peter	2 Pet.
1 John	1 John
2 John	2 John
3 John	3 John
Jude	Jude
Revelation	Rev.

OLD TESTAMENT DIVISIONS

The Pentateuch **(History)**
Genesis
Exodus
Leviticus
Numbers
Deuteronomy

Wisdom Literature
Job
Psalms
Proverbs
Ecclesiastes
Songs of Solomon

The Historical Books
Joshua
Judges
Ruth
1 Samuel
2 Samuel
1 Kings
2 Kings
1 Chronicles
2 Chronicles
Ezra
Nehemiah
Esther

The Prophetic Books
Isaiah
Jeremiah
Lamentations
Ezekiel
Daniel
Hosea
Joel
Amos
Obadiah
Jonah
Micah
Nahum
Habakkuk
Zephaniah
Haggai
Zechariah
Malachi

NEW TESTAMENT DIVISIONS

The Four Gospels
Matthew
Mark
Luke
John

The General Epistles
Hebrews
James
1 Peter
2 Peter
1 John
2 John
3 John
Jude

History
Acts

Apocalyptic Literature
Revelation

The Epistles of Paul
Romans
1 Corinthians
2 Corinthians
Galatians
Ephesians
Philippians
Colossians
1 Thessalonians
2 Thessalonians
1 Timothy
2 Timothy
Titus
Philemon

Genesis

Outline	Chapters and Verses
INTRODUCTION: Generations and Creation	1: - 4: 1- 26
Adam	5:1- 6:8
Noah and Sons	6:9 – 11:1-26
Abraham and Descendants	11: 27 - 35:1-29
Esau	36:1-4
Jacob and Descendants	37:1 – 50:26

The first Book of Moses called GENESIS

The first part of Genesis focuses on the beginning, and spread of sin in the world and culminates in the devastating flood in the days of Noah. The second part of the book focuses on God's dealing with one man, Abraham, through whom God promises to bring salvation and blessing to the world. Abraham and his descendants learn firsthand that it is always safe to trust the Lord in times of famine and feasting, blessing and bondage. From Abraham to Isaac to Jacob to Joseph; God promises begin to come to fruition in a great nation possessing a great land.

Genesis is a Greek word meaning "origin" "source," "Generation," or beginning." The original Hebrew title Bereshith means "In the Beginning."

The literary structure of Genesis is clear and is built around eleven separate units, each including the word generations
is the phrase.

Matthew

Outline	Chapters and Verses
Birth and Infancy of Messiah	
Genealogy	1: 1 – 17
Birth Of Jesus	1: 18 – 2: 18
Moved to Nazareth	2: 19 – 23
Introduction to the Messiah	
Ministry of John the Baptist	3: 1 – 3: 12
Baptism of Jesus	3: 13 – 17
Temptation of Jesus	4: 1 – 11
Abridgment of Galilean Ministry	4: 12 – 25
Dialogue I: Righteousness of The Kingdom	5: 1 – 7: 19
Narrative I: Powerful Deeds Of The Kingdom	8: 1 – 9: 38
Dialogue II: Proclamation Of The Kingdom	10: 1 – 42
Narrative II: The Presence Of The Kingdom	11: 1 – 12: 50
Dialogue III: Mystery of the Kingdom	13: 1 – 58
Narrative III: Crisis of The Kingdom	14: 1 – 17: 27
Dialogue IV: Fellowship Of The Kingdom	18: 1 – 35
Narrative IV: Conflict caused By The Kingdom	19: 1 – 23: 39
Dialogue V: Future	24: 1 – 25: 46
Passion of the Kingdom	26: 1 – 27: 66
The Resurrection	28: 1 – 20

The Gospel According to Matthew

Matthew is the gospel written by a Jew to Jews about a Jew. Matthew is the writer, his countrymen are the readings, and Jesus Christ is the subject. Matthew's design is to present Jesus as the King of the Jews, the long-awaited Messiah. Through a carefully selected series of Old Testament quotation, Matthew documents Jesus Christ's claim to be the Messiah. His genealogy, baptism, messages, and miracles all point to the same inescapable conclusion: Christ is King. Even in His death, seeming defeat is turned to victory; by the Resurrection, and the message again echoes forth: The King of the Jews lives.
At an early date this gospel was given the title Kata Matthaion, "According to Matthew." As this title suggests, other gospel account were known at that time (the word "Gospel" was added later). Matthew
("Gift of the Lord") was also surnamed Levi (Mark 2:14; Luke 5:27).

Part I

Date: ________________Day 1

Daily Reading. Chapters: Gen.1 – 7;
Ps1 – 3; Prov.1 – 3; Matt.1 – 3;

Daily Devotion. Write scriptures from your daily reading Day 1.

Make the scriptures you used personal.
How did your daily scriptures minister to you?

Date: ________________Day 2

Daily Reading. Chapters: Gen.8 – 15;
Ps. 4 – 6; Prov.4 – 6; Matt.4 – 6;

Daily Devotion. Write scriptures from your daily reading – Day 2.

Make the scriptures you used personal.
How did your daily scriptures minister to you?

Date: _______________Day 3

Daily Reading. Chapters: Gen.16 – 22;
Ps.7 – 9; Prov.7 – 9; Matt.7 – 9;

Daily Devotion. Write scriptures from your daily reading – Day 1.

Make the scriptures you used personal.
How did your daily scriptures minister to you?

Date: _______________Day 4

Daily Reading. Chapters: Gen.23 – 29;
Ps.10 – 12; Prov.10 – 12; Matt.10 – 12;

Daily Devotion. Write scriptures from your daily reading – Day 4.

Make the scriptures you used personal.
How did your daily scriptures minister to you?

Date: _______________Day 5

Daily Reading. Chapters: Gen.30 - 36;
Ps13 - 15; Prov.13 - 15; Matt.13 - 15;

Daily Devotion. Write scriptures from your daily reading - Day 5.

Make the scriptures you used personal.
How did your daily scriptures minister to you?

Date: ________________Day 6

Daily Reading. Chapters: Gen.37 - 43;
Ps.16 - 18; Prov.16 - 18; Matt.16 - 18;

Daily Devotion. Write scriptures from your daily reading - Day 6.

Make the scriptures you used personal.
How did your daily scriptures minister to you?

Date: _______________Day 7

Daily Reading. Chapters: Gen. 44 – 50;
Ps. 19 – 21; Prov.19 – 21; Matt.19 – 21;

Daily Devotion. Write scriptures from your daily reading – Day 7.

____
____
____
____
____
____
____
____
____
____
____

Make the scriptures you used personal.
How did your daily scriptures minister to you?

____
____
____
____
____
____
____
____
____
____
____
____
____
____
____
____
____
____
____
____

Exodus

Outline	Chapter and Verses
Oppression in Egypt	1: 1 - 11: 10
Redemption Out of Egypt	12:1 - 14:31
Education of the Redeemed In the Wilderness	15: 1 - 18: 27
Consecration of the Redeemed At Mt. Sinai	19: 1 - 34:35
Worship of the Redeemed In the Tabernacle, Priesthood, and Ritual	35: 1 - 40:38

The Second Book of Moses Called EXODUS

Exodus is the record of Israel's birth as a nation. Within the protective "womb" of Egypt, the Jewish family of seventy rapidly multiplies. At the right time, accompanied with severe
"birth pain," an infant nation, numbering between two and three million people, is brought into the world where it is divinely protected, fed and nurtured.

The Hebrew title, We'elleh Shemoth, "Now These Are the Names," comes from the first phrase in 1:1, Exodus begins with "Now" to show it is as a continuation of Genesis. The Greek title is Exodus, a word meaning, "exit," "departure," or "going out." The Septuagint uses this word to describe the book by its key event (read 19:1, "going forth out"). In Luke 9:31 and in Second Peter 1:15, the word exodus speaks of physical death redemption is accomplished only through death. The Latin title is Liber Exodus, "Book of Departure." Taken from the Greek title.

Mark

Outline	Chapters and Verses
The Period of Preparation	1: 1 - 13
Galilean Ministry	1: 14 - 9: 50
The Public Ministry	10: 1 - 52
The Passion Week	
Triumphal Entry	11: 1 - 11
Curse the fig tree	11: 12 - 14
Cleaning the Temple	
Faith and Fear	11: 20 - 33
Parable and Controversy	12: 1 - 44
The Olivet Discourse	13: 1 - 37
The Anointing at Bethany	14: 1 - 11
The Last Supper	14: 12 - 25
Jesus in Gethsemane	14: 26 - 52
The Jewish Trials	14: 53 - 72
The Roman Trials	15: 1 - 20
The Crucifixion and Burial	5: 21 - 47
The Resurrection	16: 1 - 20

The Gospel According to MARK

The message of Mark's gospel is captured in a single verse:
"For even the Son of man came not to be ministered unto, but to minister, and to give His life a ransom for many" (10:45).
Chapter by chapter, the book unfolds the dual focus of Christ's life: service and sacrifice.

Mark portrays Jesus as a Servant on the move, instantly responsive to the will of the Father. By preaching, teaching, and healing, He ministers to the needs of others even to the point of death. After the Resurrection, He commissions His followers to continue His work in His power - servants following in the steps of the perfect Servant.

The ancient title for this gospel was Kata Markon, "According to Mark." The author is best known by his Latin name Marcus, but in Jewish circles he was called by his Hebrew name John. Acts 12:12,, 25 refer to him as "John, whose surname was Mark."

Isaiah 40: 31
But they that wait upon the Lord shall renew
their strength; they shall mount up with wings
as eagles they shall run, and not be weary; and
they shall walk, and not faint.

Date: _______________Day 8

Daily Reading. Chapters: Ex. 1 – 7;
Ps.22 – 24; Prov.22 – 24; Matt.22 – 24;

Daily Devotion. Write scriptures from your daily reading – Day 8.

Make the scriptures you used personal.
How did your daily scriptures minister to you?

Date: ______________Day 9

Daily Reading. Chapters: Ex.8 - 12;
Ps. 25 - 27; Prov.25 - 27; Matt.25 - 28 ;

Daily Devotion. Write scriptures from your daily reading - Day 9.

____
____
____
____
____
____
____
____
____

Make the scriptures you used personal.
How did your daily scriptures minister to you?

____
____
____
____
____
____
____
____
____
____
____
____
____
____
____
____
____
____
____
____
____
____

Date: _______________Day 10

Daily Reading. Chapters: Ex.13 - 17;
Ps.28 -30; Prov.28 - 31; Mark 1 - 3;

Daily Devotion. Write scriptures from your daily reading - Day 10.

Make the scriptures you used personal.
How did your daily scriptures minister to you?

Date: ________________Day 11
Daily Reading. Chapters: Ex.18 – 22;
Ps.31 – 33; Prov.1 – 3; Mark 4 – 6;

Daily Devotion. Write scriptures from your daily reading – Day 11.

Make the scriptures you used personal.
How did your daily scriptures minister to you?

Date: ________________Day 12

Daily Reading. Chapters: Ex.23 – 27;
Ps.34 –36; Prov.4 – 4; Mark 7 – 9;

Daily Devotion. Write scriptures from your daily reading – Day 12.

____
____
____
____
____
____
____
____
____
____

Make the scriptures you used personal.
How did your daily scriptures minister to you?

____
____
____
____
____
____
____
____
____
____
____
____
____
____
____
____
____
____
____
____
____

Date: ________________Day 13

Daily Reading. Chapters: Ex.28 – 33;
Ps. 37 – 39; Prov.7 – 9; Mark 10 – 12;

Daily Devotion. Write scriptures from your daily reading – Day 13.

____
____
____
____
____
____
____
____
____
____

Make the scriptures you used personal.
How did your daily scriptures minister to you?

____
____
____
____
____
____
____
____
____
____
____
____
____
____
____
____
____
____
____
____
____

Date: _______________Day 14

Daily Reading. Chapters: Ex.34 – 40
Ps.37 – 39 Prov.10 – 12 Mark 13 – 16;

Daily Devotion. Write scriptures from your daily reading – Day 14

Make the scriptures you used personal.
How did your daily scriptures minister to you?

Luke

Outline	Chapters and Verses
The Gospel 's Summary	1: 1 – 4
Preparation for the Savior' s Assignment	
Birth of The Savior's forerunner	1:5 – 80
Birth and Childhood of Jesus	2:1 – 52
John the Baptist prepare the Way for Jesus	3:1 – 20
Baptism, Genealogy and Temptation of Jesus	3:21 – 4:13
Galilean Ministry of Jesus	4:14 – 9:50
Journey from Galilee to Jerusalem	9:51 – 19:44
The Last days of Jesus the Savior in Jerusalem, Crucifixion and Burial	19:45 – 23:56
Jesus' Resurrection and His Ascension	24:1 – 53

The Gospel According to LUKE

Luke, a physician, writes with the compassion and warmth of a family doctor as he carefully documents the perfect humanity of the Son of Man, Jesus Christ. Luke emphasizes Jesus' ancestry, birth, and early life before moving carefully and chronologically through His earthly ministry. Growing belief and growing opposition develop side by side. Those who believe are challenged to count the cost of discipleship. Those who oppose will not be satisfied until the Son of Man hangs lifeless on a cross. But the Resurrection insures that His purpose will be fulfilled: "to seek and to save that which was lost" (19:10).

Kata Loukan, "According to Luke," is the ancient title that was added to this gospel at a very early date. The Greek

Name Luke appears only three times in the New Testament

(Col. 4:14; 2 Tim. 4:11; Philem.24).

Leviticus

Outline	Chapters and Verses
Redemption:	
The Way of Access to God:	1:1 - 16: 34
Intercession by God's Ministers: Priesthood	8:1- 10: 20
Purification of God's People:	11:1 - 15:33
The Accomplishment of Reconciliation:	16:1 - 34
Holiness: The way of living for God	17:1 - 27:34
Devotional and Worship	23:1 - 25:55
Exhortation: Appeal	26:1 - 46
Voluntary Devotion Vows:	27:1 - 34

The Third Book of Moses Called LEVITICUS

Leviticus is God's guidebook for His newly redeemed people, showing them how to worship, serve, and obey a holy God. Fellowship with God through sacrifice and obedience show the awesome holiness of the God of Israel. Indeed, "Ye shall be holy: for I the Lord your God am holy' "(19:2).

Leviticus focuses on the worship and walk of the nation of God. In Exodus, Israel was redeemed and established as a kingdom of priests and a holy nation. Leviticus shows how God's people are to fulfill their priestly calling.

The Hebrew title is Wayyiqra, "And He called." The Talmid refers to Leviticus as the "law of the Priests," and the "Law of the Offerings." The Greek title appearing in the Septuagint is Leuitikon, :The Which Pertains to the Levites." From this word, the Latin Vulgate derived its name Leviticus which was adopted as the English title. This title is slightly misleading because the book does not deal with the Levites as a whole but more with the priest, a segment of the Levites.

Psalms 25: 4
Shew me thy ways, O Lord;
Teach me thy path

Psalm 37: 23
The step of a good man are ordered
By the Lord: and He delight in
his way.

Date: ________________Day 15

Daily Reading. Chapters: Lev.1 – 7;
Ps.40 – 42; Prov.13 – 15; Luke 4 – 6;

Daily Devotion. Write scriptures from your daily reading - Day 15

____
____
____
____
____
____
____
____
____
____
____

Make the scriptures you used personal.
How did your daily scriptures minister to you?

____
____
____
____
____
____
____
____
____
____
____
____
____
____
____
____
____
____
____
____

Date: ________________Day 16

Daily Reading. Chapters: Lev.8 – 15;
Ps.43 – 45; Prov.16 – 18; Luke 7 – 9;

Daily Devotion. Write scriptures from your daily reading – Day 16.

Make the scriptures you used personal.
How did your daily scriptures minister to you?

Date: ______________Day 17

Daily Reading. Chapters: Lev.16 – 21;
Ps.46 – 48; Prov.19 – 21; Luke 10 - 12 ;

Daily Devotion. Write scriptures from your daily reading – Day 17.

Make the scriptures you used personal.
How did your daily scriptures minister to you?

Date: ________________Day 18

Daily Reading. Chapters: Lev.22 - 27; Ps.49 - 51; Prov.22 - 24; Luke 13 - 15;

Daily Devotion. Write scriptures from your daily reading - Day 18

Make the scriptures you used personal.
How did your daily scriptures minister to you?

Date: ________________Day 19
Daily Reading. Chapters: Num.1 – 7;
Ps.52 – 54; Prov.25 – 27 Luke 16 – 18;

Daily Devotion. Write scriptures from your daily reading – Day 19

Make the scriptures you used personal.
How did your daily scriptures minister to you?

Numbers

Outline	Chapters and Verses
Preparation for Leaving Mount Sinai	1:1 - 10:10
Wandering in the Wilderness	0:11- 20:13
Journey into Jordan	20: 14 – 36: 13

Aaron' death,
Appointment of Moses' Successor,
Regulations for Various Offering
Laws Relating To Vows,
Settlement of Tribes beyond the Jordan,
Directions for the Division of Canaan,
Levitical Cities and Havens of Refuge and
Laws of Female Inheritance Amended

The Fourth Book of Moses Called NUMBERS

Numbers is the book of wanderings. It takes its name from the two numberings of the Israelites – the first at Mount Sinai and the second on the plains of Moab. Most of the book, however, describes Israel's experiences as they wander in the wilderness. The lesson of Numbers is clear. While it may be necessary to pass through wilderness experiences, one does not have to lives there. For Israel, an eleven – day journey became a forty-year agony.

The title of Numbers comes from the first word in the Hebrew text, Wayyedabber, "And He Said." Jewish writing, however, usually refer to it by the fifth Hebrew word I 1:1, Bemidbar, "In the Wilderness, which more nearly indicates the content of the book. The Greek title in the Septuagint is Arithmoi, "Numbers." The Latin Vulgate followed this title and translated it Liber Numeri, "Book of Numbers." These titles are based on the two numberings: the generation of Exodus (Num.1) and the generation that grew up in the wilderness and conquered Canaan (Num. 26). Numbers has also been called the "Book of the Journeying," the "Book of the Murmurings," and the "Book of Moses."

The Gospel According to JOHN

Just as a coin has two sides, both valid, so Jesus Christ has two natures, both valid. Luke presents Christ in His humanity as the Son of Man; John portrays Him in His deity as the Son of God. John's purpose is clear: to set forth Christ in His deity in order to spark believing faith in his readers. John's gospel is topical, not primarily chronological, and it revolves around seven miracles and seven "I am" statements of Christ.

Following an extended eyewitness description of the Upper Room meal and discourse, John records events leading up to the Resurrection, the final climactic proof that Jesus is who He claims to be - the Son of God.

The title of the Fourth Gospel follows the same format as the titles of the synoptic Gospels: Kata Ioannen, "According to John." As with the other, the word "Gospel" was added later. Ioannes is detived from the Hebrew name Johanan, "Yahweh Has Been Gracious."

John

Outline	Chapters and Verses
The Revelation of:	
The Word in Eternity	1: 1, 2
The Word in Creation	1: 3, 4, 9
The Revelation Word in Redemption	1: 5 - 21: 25

Opening Witness of the New Dispensation

Great Sign and Public Discourses:

The First Sign: Water into Wine

The Second Sign: Cleaning of the Temple; Feast: Passover

Nicodemus, Dispute over John the Baptist, Samaritan Woman,

The Third Sign: Healing at a Distance

Feast: Messiah in the Temple:

The Fourth Sign: Healing the Impotent Man on the Sabbath

The Fifth Sign: Feeding the Five Thousand

The Sixth Sign: Walking on the water

The Seventh Sign: Healing the Man Born Blind

The Eighth Sign: Raise Lazarus from the dead

The Passion Week	12: 12 - 19: 42
The Risen Lord and His Redeemed Family	20: 1 - 21:25

2 Timothy 2: 15
Study to show thyself approved
unto God, a workman that
neededth not to be ashamed,
rightly dividing the word of truth.

Date: _______________Day 20

Daily Reading. Chapters: Num.8 – 14;
Ps.55 – 57; Prov.28 – 31; Luke 19 – 21;

Daily Devotion. Write scriptures from your daily reading – Day 20.

Make the scriptures you used personal.
How did your daily scriptures minister to you?

Date: _______________Day 21

Daily Reading. Chapters: Num.15 - 21;
Ps.58 - 62; Prov.28 - 31; Luke 22 - 24;

Daily Devotion. Write scriptures from your daily reading - Day 21.

Make the scriptures you used personal.
How did your daily scriptures minister to you?

Date: _______________Day 22

Daily Reading. Chapters: Num.22 – 28;
Ps.63 – 65; Prov.4 – 6; John 1 – 3;

Daily Devotion. Write scriptures from your daily reading – Day 22.

Make the scriptures you used personal.
How did your daily scriptures minister to you?

Date: _______________Day 23

Daily Reading. Chapters: Num.29 – 36; Ps.66 – 68; Prov.7 – 9; John 4 – 6;

Daily Devotion. Write scriptures from your daily reading – Day 23.

Make the scriptures you used personal.
How did your daily scriptures minister to you?

Deuteronomy

Outline	Chapters and Verses
Preface and Historical Statement	1:1-5
First Address of Moses	1:6 - 4:40
Historical and Transitional Statement	4:41 - 49
Second Address of Moses	5:1 - 26:19
Third Address of Moses	27:1 - 30:20
Moses' Closing Days and Activities, A Call to Faith, Moses Turns Over Command	31:1- 34:12

The Fifth Book of Moses Called
DEUTERONOMY

Deuteronomy, Moses' "Upper Desert Discourse," consists of a series of farewell messages by Israel's 120 - year- old leader. It is addressed to the new generation destined to possess the Land of Promise - those who survived the forty years of wilderness wandering.

Like Leviticus, Deuteronomy contains a vast amount of legal detail, but its emphasis is on the layman rather than the priests. Moses reminds the generation of the importance of obedience if they are to learn from the sad example of their parents.

The Hebrew title of Deuteronomy is Haddebharim, "The Word," taken from the opening phrase in 1:1, "These be the word." The parting words of Moses to the new generation are given in oral and written form so that they will endure to all generations. Deuteronomy has been called "five - fifths of the Law" since it completes the five books of Moses. The Jewish people have also called it Mishneh Hattorah, "Repetition of the Law," which is translated in the Septuagint as To Deuteronomion Touto, "This Second Law."

Deuteronomy, however, is not a second law but an adaptation and expansion of much of the original law given on Mount Sinai. The English title comes from the Greek title Deuteronomion, "Second Law." Deuteronomy has also been appropriately called the "Book of Remembrance."

Date: ________________Day 24

Daily Reading. Chapters: Deut.1 – 7; Ps.69 – 71; Prov.10 – 12; John 7 – 9;

Daily Devotion. Write scriptures from your daily reading – Day 24.

Make the scriptures you used personal.
How did your daily scriptures minister to you?

Date: ________________Day 25

Daily Reading. Chapters: Deut.8 – 14; Ps.13 – 15; Prov.13 – 15; John 10 – 12

Daily Devotion. Write scriptures from your daily reading – Day 25.

Make the scriptures you used personal.
How did your daily scriptures minister to you?

Date: ________________Day 26

Daily Reading. Chapters: Deut.15 - 21

Ps.75 - 77; Prov.16 - 18; John 13 - 15

Daily Devotion. Write scriptures from your daily reading - Day 26.

Make the scriptures you used personal.
How did your daily scriptures minister to you?

Date: _______________Day 27

Daily Reading. Chapters: Deut.22 – 28;
Ps.78 – 80; Prov.19 – 21; John 19 – 21;

Daily Devotion. Write scriptures from your daily reading – Day 27.

____
____
____
____
____
____
____
____
____
____
____

Make the scriptures you used personal.
How did your daily scriptures minister to you?

____
____
____
____
____
____
____
____
____
____
____
____
____
____
____
____
____
____
____
____

Date: ________________Day 28

Daily Reading. Chapters: Deut.29 – 34;
Ps.81 – 83; Prov.22 – 23; Acts 1 – 3;

Daily Devotion. Write scriptures from your daily reading – Day 28.

Make the scriptures you used personal.
How did your daily scriptures minister to you?

Joshua

Outline	Chapters and Verses
Preparing For Conquest	1:1- 5:15
Conquest of Canaan	6:1 - 12:24
Dividing the Territory	13:1 - 21:24
Concluding Events	
Joshua's farewell Address And Death	23:1- 24: -33

The Book of JOSHUA

Joshua, the first of the twelve historical books (Joshua - Esther), forges a link between the Pentateuch and the remainder of Israel's history. Through three major military campaigns involving more than thirty enemy armies, the people of Israel learn a crucial lesson under Joshua's capable leadership: victory comes through faith in God and obedience to His word, rather than through military might or numerical superiority.

The title of this book is appropriately named after its central figure, Joshua. His original name Hoshea, "Salvation" (Num. 13:16). He is also called Yeshua, a shortened from of Yehoshua. This is the Hebrew equivalent of the Greek name Iesous (Jesus). Thus, the Greek title given to the book in the Septuagint is Iesous Naus, "Joshua the Son of Nun." The Latin is Liber Josue, the "Book of Joshua."

His name is symbolic of the fact that although he is the leader of the Israelite nation during the conquest, the Lord is the Conqueror.

Acts

Outlines	Chapters and Verses
Waiting for Christian Power	1: 1 - 26
The Coming of Christian Power	2: 1 - 47
Early Days of the Church	3: 1 - 12:25
Paul's First Missionary Journey	13:1 - 14:28
The Jerusalem Council	15:1 - 29
Paul's Second Missionary Journey	15:30 18:22
Paul's Third Missionary Journey	18:23 - 21:16
Paul's route to and in Rome	21:17 - 28:31

The Acts of the Apostle

Jesus' last recorded words have come to be known as the Great Commission: "Ye shall be witnesses unto me both in Jerusalem, and in all Judea, and in Samaria, and u to the uttermost part of the earth" (1:8).

The Book of Acts, written by Luke, the physician, to Theophilus as a supplement to the Gospel of Luke (Acts 1:1, cf. Luke1: 1 – 3). The Gospel of Luke relates "all that Jesus began both to do and teach" (Acts 1:1). The Acts of the Apostles, on the other hand, begins with the Ascension of Jesus and tells the story of how the gospel was spread far beyond the confines of the Jewish community to the world. The statement of Jesus in Acts 1:8, "…and ye shall be witnesses unto me both in Jerusalem, and in all Judea, and in Samaria, and unto the uttermost part of the earth," provides an excellent outline for the book.

The Book of Acts concludes rather abruptly with Paul's imprisonment in Rome. It is assumed that the reason for this unexpected closing is that Luke had recorded all the significant events known to him at that time. The date the writing of the book is generally agreed to be about A.D. 61. It is clear from certain passages within the Book of Acts that the author was with the Apostle Paul on several occasions (Acts 16: 10 – 17; 20:5 – 21:18; 7:1 – 28:16). Some people believe that Paul was referring to Luke in 2 Corinthians 8:18 when he mentions "the brother" who was praised "throughout all the churches."

Luke's purpose in writing Acts was to give a complete history of the growth of the church, but only to list those events with which he was familiar. He does not record how the gospel spread to the east and south of Palestine, or why there were always believers in Damascus before Paul arrived.

Nevertheless, the lives and ministries of the prominent individuals that Luke does include sufficiently demonstrate the shift of the evangelical concerns Christianity from Jews to Gentiles.

Date: ________________Day 29

Daily Reading. Chapters: Josh.1 - 8;
Ps.84 - 86; Prov.24 - 26 Acts 4 - 6

Daily Devotion. Write scriptures from your daily reading - Day 29.

Make the scriptures you used personal.
How did your daily scriptures minister to you?

Date: _______________Day 30

Daily Reading. Chapters: Josh.9 – 16;
Ps.87 – 89; Prov.27 – 31; Acts 7 – 9;

Daily Devotion. Write scriptures from your daily reading – Day 30.

Make the scriptures you used personal.
How did your daily scriptures minister to you?

PART II

Date: _______________Day 31
Daily Reading. Chapters: Josh.17 – 24;
Ps.90 – 92 Prov.1 – 3; Acts 10 – 12 ;

Daily Devotion. Write scriptures from your daily reading – Day 31.

Make the scriptures you used personal.
How did your daily scriptures minister to you?

Judges

Outline	Chapters and Verses
Invasion of Canaan	1:1- 2:5
Reign of the Judges	2:6 16:31
Death of Joshua,	
Oppression by the	
Philistines and	
Ammonites, and	
Deliverance by Jephthan	
Samson	
Appendices	17:1 - 21:25

The Book of JUDGES

The Book of Judges stands in stark contrast to Joshua. In Joshua an obedient people conquered the land through trust in the power of God. In Judges, however, a disobedient and idolatrous people are defeated time and time again because of their rebellion against God.

In seven distinct cycles of sin to salvation, Judges shows how Israel had set aside God's law and in its places substituted "that which was right in his own eyes" (21:25). The recurring result of abandonment from God's law is corruption from within and oppression from without. During the nearly four centuries spanned by this book, God raises up military champions to throw off the joke of bondage and to restore the nation to pure worship. But all too soon the "sin cycle" begins again as the nation's spiritual temperature grows steadily colder.

The Hebrew title is Shophetim, meaning "judges," "rulers," "deliverers," or "saviors." Shophet not only carries the idea of maintaining justice and setting disputes, but it is also used to mean "liberating" and "delivering." First the judges deliver the people; then they rule and administer justice. The Latin Vulgate called it Liber Judicum, the "Book of Judges."

Date: ________________Day 32

Daily Reading. Chapters: Judg.1 – 7;
Ps.93 – 95; Prov.4 – 5; Acts 13 – 15;

Daily Devotion. Write scriptures from your daily reading – Day 32.

Make the scriptures you used personal.
How did your daily scriptures minister to you?

Date: _______________Day 33

Daily Reading. Chapters: Judg.8 – 14;
Ps.96 – 98; Prov.6 – 9; Acts 16 – 18;

Daily Devotion. Write scriptures from your daily reading – Day 33.

Make the scriptures you used personal.
How did your daily scriptures minister to you?

Date: _______________Day 34

Daily Reading. Chapters: Judg.15 - 21;
Ps.99 - 101; Prov.10 - 12; Acts 19 - 21;

Daily Devotion. Write scriptures from your daily reading - Day 34.

___

___

___

___

___

___

___

___

___

___

___

Make the scriptures you used personal.
How did your daily scriptures minister to you?

___

___

___

___

___

___

___

___

___

___

___

___

___

___

___

___

___

___

___

___

RUTH

Outline	Chapters and Verses
Grievous Visitations	1:1-5
Far - Reaching Decisions	1:6-22
A Surprising Encounter	2:1-23
Wholehearted Dedication	3:1-18
Complete Redemption	4:18-22

The Book of Ruth

Ruth is a cameo story of loved, devotion, and redemption set in the back context of the days of the judges. It's the story of Moabite woman who forsakes her pagan heritage in order to cling to the people of Israel and to the God of Israel. Because of her faithfulness in a time of national faithlessness, God rewards her by giving her a new husband (Boaz), a son (Obed), and a priviledged position in the lineage of David and Christ (she is the great grandmother of David).

Ruth is the Hebrew title of the book. This name may be a Moabite modofication of the Hebrew word reuit, meaning "friendship" or "association." The Septuagint entitles book Routh, the Greek equivalent of the Hebrew name. The Latin title is Ruth, a transliteration of Routh.

The Epistle of Paul to the ROMANS

The Book of Romans was written by the Apostle Paul from the city of Corinth shortly after he wrote 2 Corinthians. Since it is known that the date of his arrival in Jerusalem on his third missionary journey was A.D. 58 or 59, and that he was preparing to leave for Jerusalem (R0m. 15:25, cf. Acts 20: 16), Romans is believed to have been written in the spring of A.D. 56

Although it is commonly believed that Peter founded the church at Rome, there is very little evidence for this.

Paul was writing to a predominantly gentile audience (Rom. 1:13). His concerns in writing the Book of Romans were to educate the believers in the basic doctrines related to salvation (chaps. 1 - 8) and to help them understand the unbelief of the Jews and how they benefited from it (chaps. 9 - 11). He also explained general principles of the Christian life that he wanted them to be).

ROMANS

Outline	Chapter and Verses
Introduction and Theme	1: 1- 17
Salutation	
Thanksgiving	
Theme: Justification by Faith	
The Need of the Gospel	1:18 0 3:20
Condemnation of the Gentiles	
Condemnation of the Jews	
Condemnation of all men	
Brief Statement of the Plan of Salvation: Justification by Faith	3:21 - 31
Abraham, Condemnation of Justification	4:1 - 25
Results of Justification	5:1 - 21
Rely to First Objection to Justification: It Promotes	6:1 - 8:39
Reply to Second Objection: It Annuls God's Promises	9:1 - 11:36
Practical Exhortations	12:1 - 16:27
Service in the Church and other Duties	
Political Duties	
Personal Responsibility	
Paul's Missionary Ambitions	
Personal Greeting	

Date: ________________Day 35

Daily Reading. Chapters: Ruth 1 – 4;
Ps.102 – 104; Prov.13 – 15; Acts 22 – 25;

Daily Devotion. Write scriptures from your daily reading – Day 35.

Make the scriptures you used personal.
How did your daily scriptures minister to you?

1 SAMUEL

Outline	Chapters and Verses
Samuel, Last of the Judges, First of the Prophets	1:1- 8:22
Saul, Israel's First King	9:1- 15:35
Saul' s Early Success as King,	
Rejection of Saul	
Rise of David	16:1- 31:13
Selection of David,	
David and Goliath,	
David's Exit,	
David Obtains High Priest	
David and Nabal,	
Defeat and Death of Saul and Jonathan	

The First Book of SAMUEL

The Book of First Samuel describes the transition of leadership in Israel from judges to kings. Three characters are prominent I the book: Samuel, the last judge and the first prophet; Saul, the first king of Israel; and David, the king - elect, anointed but not yet recognized as Saul's successor.

The book of First and Second Samuel were originally one book in the Hebrew Bible, known as the "Book of Samuel" or simply "Samuel." This name has been variously translated "The Name of God," "His Name Is God," "Heard of God," and Asked of God." The Septuagint divides Samuel into two books even though it is one continuous account. This division artificially breaks up the history of David. The Greek (Septuagint) title is Bibloi Basileion, "Books of Kingdoms," referring to the later kingdoms of Israel and Judah. First Samuel is called Basileion Alpha, "First Kingdom."

Second Samuel and First and Second Kings are called "Second, Thrid, and Fourth Kingdoms." The Latin Vulgate originally called the books of Samuel and Kings Libri Regum, "Books of the Kings." Later the Latin Bible combined the Hebrew and Greek titles for the first of these books, calling it Liber I Samuelis,the "First Book of Samuel," or simply "First Samuel."

Date: _______________Day 36

Daily Reading. Chapters: 1Sam.1 - 7;
Ps.105 - 107; Prov.16- 18; Acts 26 - 28;

Daily Devotion. Write scriptures from your daily reading - Day 38.

Make the scriptures you used personal.
How did your daily scriptures minister to you?

Date: _______________Day 37

Daily Reading. Chapters: 1Sam.8 – 15;
Ps.108 – 110; Prov.19 – 21; Rom.1 – 3;

Daily Devotion. Write scriptures from your daily reading – Day 37.

Make the scriptures you used personal.
How did your daily scriptures minister to you?

Date: _______________Day 38

Daily Reading. Chapters: 1Sam. 16 – 22;
Ps.111 – 113; Prov.22 – 24; Rom.4 – 6;

Daily Devotion. Write scriptures from your daily reading – Day 38

Make the scriptures you used personal.
How did your daily scriptures minister to you?

Date: ________________Day 39

Daily Reading. Chapters: 1Sam.23 – 31;
Ps.114 – 116; Prov.25 – 27; Rom.7 – 9;

Daily Devotion. Write scriptures from your daily reading – Day 39.

Make the scriptures you used personal.
How did your daily scriptures minister to you?

2 SAMUEL

Outline	Chapter and Verses
David' s Activities after Saul' s Death, Amalekite Messenger's Account Of Saul' s death,	1: 1- 4:12
David, King of Israel and Judah Ark Brought to Jerusalem, David's Desire to Build a House for God, God's Covenant with David, David's kindness to Jonathan's Son, David sin with Bathsheba, Amnon's Seduction of Tamar	5:1 – 15:6
Abslom's Rebellion	5:7- 18:5
Overthrow of Absalom and Return of David	18:6 – 24:25

The Second Book of SAMUEL

The Book of Second Samuel records the highlights of David's reign, first over the territory of Judah, and finally over the entire nation of Israel. It traces the ascension of David to the throne, his climactic sins of adultery and murder, and the shattering consequences of those sins upon his family and nation.

Read above notes on First Samuel for details on the titles of the books of Samuel. The Hebrew titles.

1 Corinthians

Outline	Chapters and Verses
Greetings and Thanksgiving	1:1 - 9
Serious Failings Reproved	1: 10 - 6:20
Paul Replies to a Letter the Corinthians sent Him	7:1 - 14:40
The Resurrections of The Body	5: 1 - 58
Conclusion	16: 1 - 24

The First Epistle of Paul the Apostle to

CORINTHIANS

Corinth, the most important city in Greek during Paul's day, was a bustling hub of worldwide commerce, degraded culture, and idolatrous religion. There Paul founded a church (Acts 18: 1 - 17), and two of his letters are addressed "Unto the church of God which is at Corinth" (1:2; 2Cor.1:1).

First Corinthans reveals the problems, pressures, and struggles of a church called out of a pagan society. Paul addresses a variety of problems in the lifestyles of the Corinthian church: factions, lawsuits, immorality, questionable practices, abuse of the Lord's Supper, and spiritual gifts. In addition to words of discipline, Paul shares words of counsel in answer to questions raised by the Corinthian believers.

The oldest recorded title of this epistle is Pros Korinthious A, in effect, the "First to the Corinthias." The "A " was no doubt a later addition to distinguish this book from Second Corinthians.

Date: ________________Day 40

Daily Reading. Chapters: 2Sam.1 - 8;
Ps.117 - 118; Prov.28 - 31; Rom.10 - 12;

Daily Devotion. Write scriptures from your daily reading - Day 40.

____
____
____
____
____
____
____
____
____
____
____

Make the scriptures you used personal.
How did your daily scriptures minister to you?

____
____
____
____
____
____
____
____
____
____
____
____
____
____
____
____
____
____
____
____

Date: _______________Day 41

Daily Reading. Chapters: 2Sam.9 - 16;
Ps.119; Prov.1 - 3; Rom.13 - 16

Daily Devotion. Write scriptures from your daily reading - Day 41.

Make the scriptures you used personal.
How did your daily scriptures minister to you?

Date: _______________Day 42

Daily Reading. Chapters: 2Sam.17 – 24;
Ps.120 – 122; Prov.4 – 6; 1Cor.1 – 3;

Daily Devotion. Write scriptures from your daily reading – Day 42.

____
____
____
____
____
____
____
____
____
____
____

Make the scriptures you used personal.
How did your daily scriptures minister to you?

____
____
____
____
____
____
____
____
____
____
____
____
____
____
____
____
____
____
____
____

2 Corinthians

Outline	Chapters and Verses
Special Greeting	1: 1 – 11
Paul's Answer to His Critics	1: 2 - 7: 16
The Collection for the Christian At Jerusalem	8: 1 – 9:15
Paul's affirms His Apostolic.	10: 1 – 13: 14

The Second Epistle of Paul the Apostle to the

CORINTHIANS

Since Paul's first letter, the Corinthian church had been swayed by false; teachers who stirred the people against Paul. They claimed he was fickle, proud, unimpressive in appearance and speech, dishonest, and unqualified as an apostle of Jesus Christ. Paul sent Titus to Cornth to deal with the difficulties, and upon his return, rejoiced to hear of the Corinthians' change of heart. Paul wrote this letter to express his thanksgiving for the repentant majority and to appeal to the rebellious minority to accept his authority. Throughout the book he defends his conduct, character, and calling as an apostle of Jesus Christ.

To distinguish this epistle from First Corinthians, it was given the title Pros Korinthious B, the "Second to the Corinthians." The "A" and "B" were probably later additions to Pros Korinthious.

Date: ________________Day 43

Daily Reading. Chapters: 1Kin.1 – 7; Ps.123 – 125; Prov.7 – 9; 1Cor.4 – 6

Daily Devotion. Write scriptures from your daily reading – Day 43.

Make the scriptures you used personal.
How did your daily scriptures minister to you?

Date: ________________Day 44

Daily Reading. Chapters: 1Kin.8 - 14;
Ps.126 - 128; Prov.10 - 12; 1Cor.7 - 9;

Daily Devotion. Write scriptures from your daily reading - Day 44.

Make the scriptures you used personal.
How did your daily scriptures minister to you?

Date: _______________Day 45

Daily Reading. Chapters: 1Kin.15 – 22;
Ps.129 – 131; Prov.13 – 15; 1Cor.10 – 12;

Daily Devotion. Write scriptures from your daily reading – Day 45.

Make the scriptures you used personal.
How did your daily scriptures minister to you?

1 Kings

Outline	Chapters and Verses
The Reign of Solomon	1: - 11: 43
David' s Death and	
Solomon's Anointing	
Solomon' pray for wisdom,	
Building of the Temple	
Visit of Queen of Sheba	
The Divided Kingdom	12:1 - 16:29
The First Period of Antagonism	
Between Judah and Israel	
The Revolt under Jeroboam	
The Period of Friendship between	
Judah and Israel	

The First Book Of The KINGS

The first half of First King traces the life of Solomon. Under his leadership Israel rises to the peak of her size and glory. Solomon's great accomplishments, including the unsurpassed splendor of the temple; which he constructs in Jerusalem, bring him worldwide fame and respect. However, Solomon's zeal for God, diminishes in his later years, as pagan wives turn his heart away from worship in the temple of God. As a result, the king with the divided heart leaves behind a divided kingdom. For the next century, the Book of First Kings traces the twin histories of two sets of kings and two nations of disobedient people who are growing indifferent to God's prophets and precepts.

Like the two books of Samuel, the two books of Kings Were originally one in the Hebrew Bible. The original title was Melechim, "Kinns", taken from the first word in 1:1, Vehamelech, "Now King." The Septuagint artificially divided the book of Kings in the middle of the story of Ahaziah into two books. It called the books of Samuel "First and Second Kingdom" ant the books of Samuel, Kings "Third and Fourth Kingdom." The Septuagint may have divided Samuel, Kings, and Chronicles into books each because the Greek required a greater amount of scroll space than did the Hebrew. The Latin title for these books is Liber Regum Tertius et Quartus, "Third and Fourth Books of Kings.

The Second Book of the KINGS

The Book of Second Kings continues the drama begun in First Kings - the tragic history of two nations on a collision course with captivity. The author systematically traces the reigning monarchs of Israel and Judah, first by carrying one nation's history forward, then retracting the same period for the other nation.

Nineteen consecutive evil kings in Israel, leading to the captivity by Assyria. The picture is somewhat brighter in Judah, where godly kings occasionally emerge to reform the evils of their predecessors. In the end, however, sin outweighs righteousness and Judah is marched off to Babylon.

Psalms 23: 5
Thou preparest a table before me in
The presence of mine enemies:
Thou anointest my head with oil;
My cup runneth over.

2 Kings

Outline	Chapters and Verses
Ahaziah of Israel (Contd.)	1:1 - 18
Elijah's Mantle falls on Elisha	2:1 - 25
Jehoram of Isreal	3:1 - 27
Stories of Elisha	4:1 - 8: 15
Johoram and Ahaziah of Judah	8:16 - 29
Period of Renewed Antagonism Between Judah and Israel	9:1 - 17:41
Jehu of Israel, Founder of the fifth Dynasty	9:1 - 10:36
Athaliah, Queen of Judah	11: 1 - 21
Joash of Judah	12: 1 - 21
Jehoahaz and Jehoash of Israel	13: 1 - 25
Amazial of Judah	14: 1 - 22
Jeroboam II of Israel	14: 23 - 29
Uzziah (Azariah) of Judah	15: 1 - 7
Day of Chaos in Israel	15: 8 - 31
Jotham and Ahaz of Judah	15:32 - 16:20
Hoshea of Israel	17:1 - 41
The Single Kingdom - Judah, After the Collapse of Israel	
Hezekiah of Judah	18:1 - 20:1 - 21
Manasseh and Amon of Judah	21: 1 - 21
Josiah of Judah	22:1 - 23:30
The Last Day of Judah	23:31 - 25:21
Gedaliah	25:22 - 26
A Final Note	25:27–30

Date: ________________Day 46

Daily Reading. Chapters: 2Kin.1 – 7;
Ps.132 – 134; Prov.16 – 18; 1Cor.13 – 16;

Daily Devotion. Write scriptures from your daily reading – Day 46.

Make the scriptures you used personal.
How did your daily scriptures minister to you?

Date: ______________ Day 47

Daily Reading. Chapters: 2Kin.8 – 13;
Ps.135 – 137; Prov.19 – 21; 2Cor.1 – 3;

Daily Devotion. Write scriptures from your daily reading – Day 47.

Make the scriptures you used personal.
How did your daily scriptures minister to you?

Date: ________________Day 48

Daily Reading. Chapters: 2Kin.14 – 19; Ps.138 – 140; Prov.22 – 24; 2Cor.4 – 6;

Daily Devotion. Write scriptures from your daily reading – Day 48.

Make the scriptures you used personal.
How did your daily scriptures minister to you?

Date: ________________Day 49

Daily Reading. Chapters: 2Kin.20 – 25;
Ps.141 – 145; Prov. 25 – 27; 2Cor.7 – 9;

Daily Devotion. Write scriptures from your daily reading – Day 49.

____
____
____
____
____
____
____
____
____
____
____

Make the scriptures you used personal.
How did your daily scriptures minister to you?

____
____
____
____
____
____
____
____
____
____
____
____
____
____
____
____
____
____
____
____

1 Chronicles

Outline	Chapter and Verses
The Genealogies	
Of the Human – Race	1: 1 – 2:22
Of Judah	2: 3 – 4:23
Of Simeon, Reuben, Gad, Manasseh,	4: 24 – 5: 26
Of Levi: their Dwellings	6: 1 – 81
Of Issachar, Benjamin, ` Naphtali	7: 1 – 40
West Manasseh, Ephraim, And Asher	
Further Genealogies of Benjamin Including Saul	8: 1 – 9: 44
The Reign of David	
Fall of Saul' s House	10: 1 – 14
David and Valiant Men	11:1 – 12:40
Uzzah Smitten on Touching The Ark	13: 1 – 14
David' s House, Family And Victories	14: 1 – 17
The Ark Removed to Jerusalem: Arrangements of Worship	15:1 – 16:43
David' s Purpose to Build	17:1 – 27
A House for God	
David' s Engages in various	8:1 – 20:8
WarsThe Sin of Numbering The People	21:1 – 30
David Prepares for Building Of the Temple (C0NTD.)	22:1 – 19
Arrangement for Service In the Temple	23:1 – 26:32
Levit Offices of State: David's Last Acts	27:1 – 26:32

The First Book of the CHRONICLES

The books of First and Second Chronicles cover the same period of Jewish history described in Second Samuel through Second Kings, but the perspective is different. These books are no mere repetition of the same material, but rather form a divine editorial on the history of God's people. While Second Samuel, First, and Second Kings give a political history of Israel and Judah, First and Second Chronicles present a religious history of the Davidic dynasty of Judah. The former are written from a peophetic and moral viewpoint, and the latter from a priestly and spiritual perspective. The Book of First Chronicles begins with the royal line of David and then traces the spiritual significance of David's righteous reign.

The books of First and Second Chronicles were originally one continuous work in the Hebrew. The title was Dibere
Hayyamim, meaning "The Words [accounts, events] of the Days." The equivalent into two parts in the third - century
B.C.; Greek translation of the Hebrew Bible (the Septuagint). At that time it was given the name Paraleipomenon, "Of Things Omitted." Referring to the things ommited from Samuel and Kings. Some copies add thr phrase, Basileon Iouda, "Concerning the Kings of Judah." The first of Chronicles was called Paraleipomenon Primus, "The First Book of Things Omitted." The name "Chronicles" comes from Jerom in his Latin Vulgate Bible (A.D. 385 - 405): Chronicorum Liber. He meant his in the sense of the Chronicles of the Whole of Sacred History

The Epistle of Paul the Apostle to the GALATIANS

The Galatians, having launched their Christian experience by faith, seem content to leave their voyage of faith and chart a
New course based on works - a course Paul finds disturbing. His letter to the Galatians is a vigorous attack against the gospel of works and a defense of the gospel of faith.

Paul begins by setting forth his credentials as an apostle with a message from God: blessing comes from God on the basis of faith, not law. The law declares men guilty and imprisons them; faith sets men free to enjoy liberty in Christ. But liberty is not license. Freedom in Christ in Christ means freedom to produce the fruits of righteousness through a Spirit - led lifestyle.

The book is called Pros Galatas, "To the Galatians," and it is the only letter of Paul that is specifically addressed to a number of churches ("unto the churches of Galatia," 1:2). The name was given to this Celtic people because they originally
Lived in Gaul before their migration to Asia Minor.

Galatians

Outline	Chapters and Verses
Introduction	
Paul's Greeting to the Galatians	1: 1 – 5
Occasion for Writing: their fall From the Gospel	1: 6 – 9
Paul's Authority and the Authenticity Of His Message	
Paul's Gospel Revealed: To Him by Jesus	1: 10 – 24
Paul's acknowledgment By other Apostles	2: 1 – 10
Paul Correct s Peter; Wrong Teaching	2: 11 – 21
The Way of Salvation	
Salvation in Christ Jesus: By Faith, not by Works	3: 1 – 14
Salvation in Christ Jesus; Through Promise, Not the Law	3: 15 – 22
Those who trust in Jesus: become Sons, not Slaves	2: 23 – 4: 7
Expostulation	4: 8 – 20
The Path of Freedom	5: 1 – 6: 10
Sacrificial Living in Contrast to Legalism	6: 11 – 18

Date: _______________Day 50

Daily Reading. Chapters: 1Chr.1 – 7;
Ps.144 – 146; Prov. 28 – 31; 2Cor.10 – 13;

Daily Devotion. Write scriptures from your daily reading – Day 50.

____
____
____
____
____
____
____
____
____
____
____

Make the scriptures you used personal.
How did your daily scriptures minister to you?

____
____
____
____
____
____
____
____
____
____
____
____
____
____
____
____
____
____
____

Date: ________________Day 51

Daily Reading. Chapters: 1Chr.8 – 14;
Ps. 147 – 150; Prov.1 – 3 Gal.1 – 3;

Daily Devotion. Write scriptures from your daily reading – Day 51.

Make the scriptures you used personal.
How did your daily scriptures minister to you?

Date: ________________Day 52

Daily Reading. Chapters: 1Chr.15 – 21;
Ps.1 – 3 Prov.4 – 6; Gal.4 – 6

Daily Devotion. Write scriptures from your daily reading – Day 52.

Make the scriptures you used personal.
How did your daily scriptures minister to you?

Date: ________________Day 53

Daily Reading. Chapters: 1Chr.22 – 29;
Ps.4 – 6; Prov.7 – 9; Eph.1 – 3;

Daily Devotion. Write scriptures from your daily reading – Day 53.

____

____

____

____

____

____

____

____

____

____

____

Make the scriptures you used personal.
How did your daily scriptures minister to you?

____

____

____

____

____

____

____

____

____

____

____

____

____

____

____

____

____

____

____

____

2 Chronicles

Outline	Chapters and Verses
The Reign Of Solomon	1:1 - 9:31
Solomon Confirmed in he Kingdom:	
Build the Temple	1:1 - 4:22
The Ark Removed to Temple:	5:1 - 7:22
Solomon' s Address and Prayer	
Acts of Solomon and his Glory	8:1 - 9:31
The Kingdom f Judah	
Rehoboam and the Revolt Of the Ten Tribes	10:1 - 11:23
Abijah at War with Jeroboam	13:1 -22
Asa Opposes Idolatry:	14:1 - 15: 9
Asa' s Conflict with Bassha:	16: 1 - 14
Jehoshapht Prospers:	17:1 - 18:34
Jehoshapht Starts. Reforms and Blessed	19:1 - 20:37
Jehoram chastised of His sins	21:1 - 20
Ahaziah' s Evil Reign of Sins	2:1 - 12
Jehoiada Makes Joash King	23:1 - 21
Reign of Joash	24:1 - 27
Reign of Amaziah	25:1 - 28
Reign of Uzziah:	26:1 - 23
Reign of Jotham:	27:1 - 9
Reign of Ahaz:	28:1 - 27
Reign of Hezekiah	29:1 - 32:32
Manasseh and Ammon:	33: 1 - 25
Reign of Josiah:	34:1 - 35:27
Last Kings of Judah	36:1 - 23

The Second Book of the CHRONICLES

The Book of Second Chronicles parallels First and Second Kings but virtually ignores the northern kingdom of Israel because of its false worship and refusal to acknowledge the temple in Jerusalem. Chronicles focuses on those kings who pattern their lives and reigns after the life and reign of godly King David. It gives extended treatment to such zealous reformers as Asa, Jehoshaphat, Joash, Hezekiah, and Josiah.

The temple and temple worship, central throughout the book, befit a nation whose worship of God is central to its very survival. The book begins with Solomon's glorious temple and concludes with Cyrus' edict to rebuild the temple more than four hundred years later.

Ephesians

Outline	Chapters and Verses
Salutation	1: 1 – 2
Thanksgiving for the Glorious Plan of Salvation	
God's Plain for the Church; Holiness, Grace, and Glory	1: 3 – 6
Jesus' Redemption, United All in Him	1: 7 – 12
The Holy Spirit's Seal, Example, And Pledge of Inheritance	1: 13 – 14
Prayer that Christian Correspond to Divine Provision	1: 15 – 23
The Unity of the believer In Christ	2: 1 – 3: 21
Exhortation to Walk as Christian	4: 1 – 6: 9
Exhortation to be Strong in The Lord	6: 10 – 17
Exhortation to Pray: Benedictory	6: 18 – 24

The Epistle of Paul the Apostle to the EPHESIANS

Ephesus was the capital of the chief province of Asia. It was located about one mile from the Aegean Sea. The temple of Diana (Artemis) was important to the commerce of the city because the Mediterranean world considered it to be such a sacred and impeccable institution, that it became the chief banking establishment in all of Asia Minor. The great number of pilgrims that came to worship at the temple also bolstered the economy in Ephesus. In fact, the population is believed to have exceeded a quarter million.

Paul came to Ephesus during his second missionary journey with Aquila and Priscilla but journeyed on to Jerusalem by himself (acts 18: 18 - 21).

On his next missionary journey, Paul spent three years in Ephesus (Acts 19:). He had so much influence on the people there that the craftsman who manufactured silver shrines for Diana incited a riot against him, concerned that their trade would become obsolete (Acts 19: 24 - 29).

The Book of Ephesians was probsbly written by Paul during his important in Rome (ca. A.D. 60 - 64) about the same time he wrote Colossians and Philemon. The content of the of Ephesians is very similar to the of Colossians; both stress doctrin and give instruction in practical Christian duties. One difference between them, however, is that Colossians portrays Christ as the head of the Church, while Ephesians goes on display Jesus as the ascended, glorified Christ.

The major theme of tis letter is that the Church (ekklesia [1577]) is the body of Christ (Eph.1: 22, 23, 2:15, 16). Paul also metaphorically spoke of the Church as a bride who will soon be united with Christ (Eph.5:21 - 33). The key idea is that a body has individual parts that must operate as a unit. God's plan is to bring all believes together (Eph.1: 10) with Christ as the head (Eph.1:22, 23).

Date: _______________Day 54

Daily Reading. Chapters: 2Chr.1 – 7;
Ps.7 – 9; Prov. 10 – 12; Eph.4 – 6;

Daily Devotion. Write scriptures from your daily reading – Day 54.

Make the scriptures you used personal.
How did your daily scriptures minister to you?

Philippians

Outline	Chapters and Verses
Greeting	1: 1 - 2
Thanksgiving and Prayer for Philippians	1: 3 - 11
For Paul to Live in Christ: Paul's Attitude Reflects Christ	1: 12 - 4: 1
Exhortation: Plea for Unity and Peace Concluding Testimony and Repeated Thanks Greeting and Benediction	4: 2 - 23

The Epistle of Paul to the PHILIPPIANS

Paul writes a thank - you note to the believers at Philippi for their help in his hour of need, and he uses the occasion to send along some instruction on Christian unity. His central thought is simple: Only in Christ are real unity and joy possible. With Jesus Christ as your model of humility and service, you can enjoy a oneness of purpose, attitude, goal, and labor - a true which Paul illustrates from his own life, and one the Philippians desperately need to hear.

This epistle is called Pros Phillippesious. "To the Philippians." The church at Philippi was the first church Paul founded in Mecedonia.

The city of Philippi was named for Philip of Mecedon, the father of Alexander the Great, who seized the city in 358 B.C. from the Thracians.

Date: ________________Day 55

Daily Reading. Chapters: 2Chr.8 – 14;
Ps.10 – 12; Prov. 13 – 15; Phil.1 – 4;

Daily Devotion. Write scriptures from your daily reading – Day 55.

Make the scriptures you used personal.
How did your daily scriptures minister to you?

Colossians

Outline	Chapters and Verses
Greeting	1: 1 - 2
Thanksgiving	1: 3 - 8
Prayer	1: 9 - 12
God's Word in Christ Jesus Redemption The Excellence of Christ Reconciliation	1: 13 - 23
Paul's Ministry	1: 24 - 2: 3
False Teaching Denounced	2: 4 - 23
The Christian Life	3: 1 - 4: 6
Conclusion	4: 7 - 9

The Epistle of Paul the Apostle to the
COLOSSIANS

If Ephesians can be labeled the epistle portraying the "church of Christ," then Colossians must surely be the "Christ of the church." Ephesians focuses on the body; Colossians focuses on the Head. Like Ephesians, the little Book of Colossians divides neatly in half with the first portion doctrinal (1 and 2) and the second practical (3 and 4). Paul's purpose is to show that Christ is preeminent - first and foremost in everything and the Christian's life should reflect that priority. Because believers are rooted in Him, alive in Him, hidden in Him. Clothed in His love, with His peace ruling in their hearts, they are equipped to make Christ first in every area of life.

This epistle became known as Pros Kolossari, "to the Colossians," because of 1:2. Paul also wanted it to be read in the neighboring church at Laodicea (4:16).

Date: _____________Day 56

Daily Reading. Chapters: 2Chr.15 – 21;
Ps.13 – 15; Prov.16 – 18; Col.1 – 4;

Daily Devotion. Write scriptures from your daily reading – Day 56.

Make the scriptures you used personal.
How did your daily scriptures minister to you?

1 Thessalonians

Outline	Chapters and Verses
Relation of Paul to the Thessalonians Church	
Response of the Gospel	1: 2- 10
Prayer of Thanksgiving	
Proofs of Election	
Recounting of the Character Of Paul's Ministry	2: 1 – 12
Reception by the Thessalonians	2: 13 – 16
Relation of Paul with Thessalonians	2: 17 – 3: 13
Exhortation of Paul to the Church	4: 1 – 5: 28
Concerns of the Believers	5: 12 – 22
The Rapture of the Saints	
The Day of the Lord	
Conduct of the Church	
Concluding Prayer	5: 23 – 24
Final Request	5: 25 – 28

The First Epistle of Paul the Apostle to the
THESSALONIANS

Paul has many pleasant memories of the days he spent with the infant Thessalonian church. Their faith, hope, love, and perseverance in the face of persecution are exemplary. Paul's labors as a spiritual parent to the fledgling church have been richly rewarded, and his affection is visible in every line of his letter.

Paul encourages them to excel in their newfound faith, to increase in their love for one another, and to rejoice, pray, and give thanks always. He closes his letter with instruction regarding the return of the Lord, whose advent signifies hope and comfort for believes both living and dead.

This is the first of Paul's two canonical letters to the church at Thessalonica, it received the title Pros Thessalonkeis A, the "First to the Thessalonians."

Date: ________________Day 57

Daily Reading. Chapters: 2Chr.22 – 28;
Ps.16 – 18; Prov.19 – 21; 1Thess.1 – 5;

Daily Devotion. Write scriptures from your daily reading – Day 57.

Make the scriptures you used personal.
How did your daily scriptures minister to you?

Psalm 35: 27,

Let them shout for joy, and be gald, that favour my righteous cause: yea let them say continually, Let the Lord be magnified, which hath pleasure in the prosperity of his servant.

Jesus Is the Way; The Only way!

2 Thessalonians

Outline	Chapters and Verses
Introduction	1: 1 – 12
Salutation	
Thanksgiving	
Intercession	
Instruction of the Thessalonians Believers:	2: 1 – 17
Correction of a Misconception	
Revelation of the Man of Sin	
His Character	
His Restrainer	
His Ministry	
Judgment of Unbelievers	
Thanksgiving and Prayer	
Injunctions to the Thessalonians Believers:	3: 1 – 16
Call to Prayer15	
Discipline in the Assembly	
Salutation	3: 17 – 18

The Second Epistle of Paul the Apostle to the THESSALONIANS

Since Paul's first letter, the seeds of false doctrine have been sown among the Thessalonians, causing them to waver in their faith. Paul removes these destructive seeds and again plants the seeds of truth. He begins by commending the believes on their faithfulness in the midst of persecution and encouraging them that present suffering will be repaid with future glory. Therefore, in the midst of persecution, expectation can be high.

Paul then deals with the central matter of his letter: a misunderstanding spawned by false teachers regarding the coming day of the Lord. Despite events that must first take place. Laboring for the gospel, rather than lazy resignation, is the proper response.

As the second letter in Paul's Thessalonian correspondence, this was entitled Pros Thessalonikeis B, the "Second to the Thessalonians.

Date: ________________Day 58

Daily Reading. Chapters: 2Chr.28 – 38;
Ps.19 – 21; Prov.22 – 24; 2Thess.1 – 3;

Daily Devotion. Write scriptures from your daily reading – Day 58.

Make the scriptures you used personal.
How did your daily scriptures minister to you?

Ezra

Outline	Chapters and Verses
Return of the Exiles from: Babylon to Jerusalem	1: 1 - 11
The Register of Those who Returned	2: 1 - 70
Building of the Altar And the Temple Foundation	3: 1 - 13
Cessation of the Work Through Opposition	4: 1 - 24
Completion of the Temple	5: 1 - 6: 22
Ezra' s Mission	8: 1 - 36
The Problem of Mixed Marriages	9: 1 - 10:44

The Book of EZRA

Ezra continues the Old Testament narrative of Second Chronicles by showing how God fulfills His promise to return His people, to the Land of Promise after seventy years of exile. Israel's second exodus," this one from Babylon, is less impressive than the return from Egypt because only a remnant chooses to leave Babylon.

Ezra relates the story of two returns from Babylon - the first led by Zerubbable to rebuild the temple (1 - 6), and the second under the leadership of Ezra to rebuild the spiritual condition of the people (7 - 10). Sandwiched between these two accounts is a gap of nearly six decades, during which Esther lives and rules as queen in Persia.

Ezra is Aramaic form of the Hebrew word ezer, "help," and perhaps means "Yahweh helps. "Ezra and Nehemiah were originally bound together as one book because Chronicles, Ezra and Nehemiah were viewed as one continuous history.

The Septuagint, a Greek - language version of the Old Testament translated in the third century B.C., calls Ezra - Nehemiah, Esdras Deuteron, "Second Esdras." Frist Esdras is the name of the apocryphal book of Esdras. The Latin title is Liber Primus Esdrae, "The First Book of Ezra," In the Latin Bible, Ezra is called First Ezra and Nehemiah is called Second Ezra.

The First Epistle of Paul the Apostle to TIMOTHY

Paul, the aged and experienced apostle, writes to the young pastor Timothy who is facing a heavy burden of responsibility in the church at Ephesus. The task is challenging: false doctrine must be erased, public worship safeguarded, and mature leadership developed. In addition to the conduct of the church, Paul talks pointedly about the conduct of the minister. Timothy must be on his guard lest his youthfulness become a liability, rather than an asset, to the gospel. He must be careful to avoid false teachers and greedy motives, pursuing instead righteousness, godliness, faith, love, perseverance, and the gentleness that befits a man of God.

The Greek title for this is Pros Timtheon A, the "First to Timothy." Timothy means "honoring God" or honored by God," and probably was given to him by his mother Eunice.

1 Timothy

Outline	Chapters and Verses
Greeting	1: 2
The Circumstances at Ephesus	1: 3 – 17
The Charge to Timothy	1: 18 – 20
Directions Concerning Public Worship	2: 1 – 15
Qualification of Church Officers Bishops and Deacons	3: 1 – 13
Purpose of the Church	3: 14 – 16
Instruction Concerning Apostasy	4: 1 – 16
Instruction Concerning Groups and Individuals in the Church: Older and Younger Men and Women Widows Elders and Prospective Elder Slaves False Teachers A Concluding Appeal	5: 1 – 6: 21

The Book of NEHEMIAH

Nehemiah, contemporary of Ezra and cupbearer to the king in the Persian palace, leads the third and last return to Jerusalem after thr Babylonian exile. His concer for the welfare of Jerusalem and its inhabitants prompts him to take bold action. Granted permission to return to his homeland. Nehemiah challenges his countrymen to arise and rebuild the shattered wall of Jerusalem. In spite of opposition from without and abuse from within. The task is completed in only fifty - two days, a task even the enemies of Israel must attribute to God's enabling. By contrast, the task of reviving and reforming the people of God within the rebuilt wall demands years of Nehemiah's godly life and leadership.

The Hebrew for Nehemiah is Nehemyah, "Comfort of Yahweh." The book is named after its chief character, whose name appears in the opening nerse. Thecombined book of Ezra - Nehemiah is given the Greek title Esdras Deuteron, "Second Esdras" in the Septuaging, a third - century B.C. Greek -

Language: translation of the Hebrew Old Testament. The Latin title of Nehemiah is Liber Secundus Esdrae, "Second Book of Ezra, and is later called Liber Nehemiae, "Book of Nehemiah.

Nehemiah

Outline	Chapters and Verses
Nehemiah's Prayer over Jerusalem's Distress	1: 1 – 11
Nehemiah' s Return to Jerusalem as Governor	2: 1 – 11
Plan To Rebuild The City Wall	2: 12 – 20
Building Of The Wall	3: 1 – 32
Threats to the Building	
Discouraging Sarcasm	4: 1 – 6
Enemy Attacks	4: 7 – 23
Disunity Within	5: 1 – 19
False Accusation	6: 1 – 14
The Wall Completion	6:15 – 7:4
Register of the Returned Exiles	7:5 – 73
The Reading and Exposition Of the Law	8: 1 – 18
Prayer of Repentance and Covenant of Obedience	9:1 – 10:39
Register of the Inhabitants of	11: 1 – 12: 26
Dedication of the Walls	12:27 – 47
Nehemiah' s Reforms	13:1 – 31

Date: _______________Day 59

Daily Reading. Chapters: Ezra 1 – 10;
Ps.22; Prov.25; 1Tim.1 – 3;

Daily Devotion. Write scriptures from your daily reading – Day 59.

Make the scriptures you used personal.
How did your daily scriptures minister to you?

Date: _______________Day 60

Daily Reading. Chapters: Neh.1 – 13;
Ps. 23; Prov. 26; 1Tim.4 – 6;

Daily Devotion. Write scriptures from your daily reading – Day 60.

Make the scriptures you used personal.
How did your daily scriptures minister to you?

Esther

Outline	Chapters and Verses
Vashti Demoted	1; 1 – 22
Esther Promoted	2: 1 – 23
Haman's Rage	3: 1 – 15
Esther' s Stage	4: 1 – 5: 8
Haman Hanged	5: 9 – 7: 10
Mordecai and Esther Elevated	8: 1 – 10: 3

The Book of ESTHER

God's hand of providence and protection on behalf of His people is evident throughout the Book of Esther, through His name does not appear once. Haman's plot brings great danger to the Jews and is countered by the courage of beautiful Esther and the cousel of her wise cousin Mordecai, resulting in a great deliverance. The Feast of Purim becomes an annual reminder of God's faithfulness on behalf of His people.

Esther's Hebrew name was Hadassah, "Myrle" (2:7), but her Persian name Ester was derived from the Persian word for "Star" (Stara). The Greek title was book is Esther, and the Latin title is Hester.

2 Timothy

Outline	Chapters and Verses
Introduction	1: 1 – 5
Salutation	
Thanksgiving	
First Charge:	1: 6 – 18
Rekindle your Gift	
Be Willing to Suffer	
Paul's Example	
Guard the Truth	
Paul's Present Circumstances	
Second Charge:	2: 1 – 13
Be Strong	
Pass on the Message to Faithful Men	
Example of Soldier, Athlete, and Farmer	
Jesus Christ, the Inspiration for Steadfastness	
Third Charge:	
Avoid Vain Disproving and Senseless Controversies	
Warning of Approaching Apostasy	
Continue in the Faith	
Fourth Charge:	
Preach the Word	
Paul's Triumphant Confession	
Personal Instruction and Information	4:9 – 19
Concluding Greeting and Benediction	4:20 – 22

PART III

Date: ________________Day 61

Daily Reading. Chapters: Esther 1 - 10;
Ps. 24; Prov.27; 2Tim.1 - 4;

Daily Devotion. Write scriptures from your daily reading - Day 61.

Make the scriptures you used personal.
How did your daily scriptures minister to you?

Titus

Outline	Chapters and Verses
Salutation to Titus	1: 1 – 4
General Instructions for Reforming Church Life in Christ Jesus:	1: 5 – 16
Qualifications for Elder Leadership	
Warning against Unhealthy Judaizing Influences	
Instructions for Preaching to the People:	2: 1 – 15
Moral Responsibilities of Christian	
Necessary Relationship of Salvation to Personal Ethics	
Concluding Instruction for Christian In the World:	3: 1 – 15
Civil and Social Responsibilities Of Christian	
God's Power to save any Sinner Through Christ	
Preach the Gospel and not with Legalists	
Closing Requests: Personal	

The Epistle of Paul the Apostle to TITUS

Tirus, a young pastor, faces the unenviable assignment of setting in order the church at Crete. Paul writes advising him to appoint elders, men of proven spiritual character in their homes and businesses, to oversee the work of the church. But elders are not the only individuals in the church who are required to excel spiritually. Men and women, young and old, each have their vital functions to fulfill in the church if they are to be living examples of the doctrine they profess. Throughout his letter to Titus, (Contd.)
Paul stresses the necessary, practical working out of salvation in the daily lives of both the elders and congregation. God works are desirable and profitable for all believers.

This third Pastoral Epistle is simply titled Pros Titon, "To Titus." This was also the name of the Roman general who destroyed Jerusalem in A.D. 70 and succeeded his father Vespasian as emperor.

Job

Outline	Chapters and Verses
Prologue	
Character of Job	1: 1 – 5
Misfortune of Job	1: 6 – 2: 10
Friends of Job	2: 11 – 13
The Three Friends' Solution	
First Cycle of Speeches	3: 1 – 14: 22
Second Cycle of Speeches	15: 1 – 21: 34
Third Cycle of Speeches	22: 1 – 3: 40
Elihu' s Solution	32: 1 – 37: 24
The Lord' s Solution	
First Speech	38: 1 – 40:2
Job' s Response	40: 3 – 5
Second Speech	40: 6 – 41: 34
Job' s Response	42: 1 – 6
Epilogue	
The Lord Rebuke the Three Friends	42: 7 – 9
The Lord' s Restoration of Job	42: 10 – 17

The Book of JOB

Job is perhaps the earliest book of the Bible. Set in the period of the patriarchs (Abraham, Isaac, Jacob, and Joseph), it tells the story of a man who loses everything – his wealth, his family, his health and wrestles with the question, Why?

The book begins with a heavenly debate between God and Satan, moves through three cycles of earthly debates between Job and his friends, and concludes with a dramatic "divine diagnosis" of Job's problem. In the end, Job acknowledges the sovereignty of God in his life and receives back more he had before his trials.

Iyyob is the Hebrew title for this book, and the name has two possible meanings. If derived from the Hebrew word for "Persecution," it means "Persecuted One." It is more likely that it comes from the Arabic word meaning "To Come Back"
Or "Repent." If so, it may be defined "Repentant One." Both meaning apply to the book. The Greek title is Iob, and the Latin is Iob.

Date: ________________Day 62

Daily Reading. Chapters: Job 1 – 7;
Ps.25 – 27 Prov.28 – 31 Titus 1 – 3;

Daily Devotion. Write scriptures from your daily reading – Day 62.

Make the scriptures you used personal.
How did your daily scriptures minister to you?

Date: _______________Day 63

Daily Reading. Chapters: Job 8 – 14;
Ps. 28 –31; Prov.1 – 3; Philemon

Daily Devotion. Write scriptures from your daily reading – Day 63.

Make the scriptures you used personal.
How did your daily scriptures minister to you?

Date: ________________Day 64

Daily Reading. Chapters: Job 15 – 21;
Ps.32 – 34; Prov.4 – 6; Heb.1 – 4;

Daily Devotion. Write scriptures from your daily reading – Day 64.

Make the scriptures you used personal.
How did your daily scriptures minister to you?

Date: _______________Day 65

Daily Reading. Chapters: Job 22 – 28;
Ps.35 – 37; Prov.7 – 9; Heb.5 – 10;

Daily Devotion. Write scriptures from your daily reading – Day 65.

Make the scriptures you used personal.
How did your daily scriptures minister to you?

Date: _______________Day 66

Daily Reading. Chapters: Job 29 – 35;
Ps.38 – 40; Prov.10 – 12; Heb.11 – 13;

Daily Devotion. Write scriptures from your daily reading – Day 66.

Make the scriptures you used personal.
How did your daily scriptures minister to you?

Philemon

Outline	Chapters and Verses
Title and Salutation	1 - 3
Thanksgiving for Philemon' s Love and Faith	4 - 7
Plea for Onesimus	8 - 12
Paul's Consideration in Sending Back Onesimus	13 - 16
Appeal to Philemon to Receive Onesimus	17 - 21
Personal Matters: Greetings	22 - 25

The Epistle of Paul the Apostle to PHILEMON

Does Christian brotherly love rally work, even in situations of extraordinary tension and difficulty? Will it work, for example, between a prominent slaver owner and one of his runaway slaves? Paul has no doubt! He writes a "postcard" to Philemon, his beloved brother and fellow worker, on behalf of Onesimus - a deserter, thief, and formerly worthless slave. But now Philemon's brother in Christ with much tact and tenderness, Paul asks Phiemon to receive Onesimus back with the same gentleness with which he would receive Paul himself. Any debt Onesimus owes Paul promises to make good.

Knowing Phiemon, Paul is confident that brotherly love and forgiveness will carry the day.

Since this letter is addressed to Philemon in verse 1, it becomes known as Pros Philemona, "To Philemon." Like First and Second Timothy and Titus, it is addressed to an individual, but unlike the Pastoral Epistles, Philemon ia also address to a family and church (v.2).

Hebrews

Outline	Chapter and Verses
Preface: Course and High Point Of Divine Revelation	1: 1 - 3
The Supremacy of Christ Jesus Himself	1: 4 - 4: 13
Superiority of Jesus to Angels	
Warning of Indifference to These Truths	
The Reason Jesus Became Human	
Jesus' is greeting than that of Moses	
Warning about Unbelief	
The Priesthood of Christ Jesus	4:14 - 10:18
Perseverance of Christians	10:19 - 12:29
Exhortation and Benediction	13:1 - 25

The Epistle of Paul the Apostle to the HEBREWS

Many Jewish believers, having stepped out of Judaism into Christianity, want to reverse their course in order to escape persecution by their countrymen. The write of Hebrews exhorts them to "go on unto perfection: (6:1). His appeal is based on the superiority of Christ over the Judaic system. Christ is better than the angels, for they worship Him.
He is better than Moses, for He created him. He is better than the Aaronic priesthood, for His sacrifice was once for all time. He is better than the law, for He mediates a better covenant. In short, there is more to be gained in Christ than to be lost in Judaism. Pressing on in Christ produces tested faith, self - discipline, and visible love seen in good works

Although the King James Version uses the title "The Epistle of Paul the Apostle to the Hebrew," there is no early manuscript evidence to support it. The oldest and most reliable title is simply Pros Ebraious, "To Hebrew."

James

Outline	Chapters and Verses
God's Purpose for the Believer's Advancement in Unadulterated Faith	1: 1 – 27
Test Of Pure Faith	2: 1 – 5: 20
True and False Confidence	
Fleshly and Spiritual Self	
Faith Operative through Love	
Love as an Approach to Life	
Selfish Faction	
Self – Willed Life Direction	
Charity in the Acquisition and Stewardship of Wealth	
Patience under Oppression	
Restraint in Commitments	
Prevailing Prayer	

The Epistle of JAMES

Faith without works cannot be called faith. "Faith without works is dead" (2:26), and a dead faith is worse than no faith at all. Faith must work; it must produce; it must be visible. Verbal faith is not enough; mental faith is insufficient. Faith must be there, but it must be more. It must inspire action. Throughout his epistle to Jewish believers< James integrates true faith and everyday practical experience by stressing that true faith must manifest itself in works of faith.

Faith endures trails. Trials come and go, but a strong faith will face them head on and develop endurance. Faith understands temptations. It will allow us to consent to our lust and slide into sin. Faith harbors no prejudice. For James, faith and favoritism cannot coexist. Faith displays itself in works. Faith is more than mere words; it is more than knowledge; it is demonstrated by obedience; and it overtly responds to the promises of God. Faith controls the tongue. This small but immensely powerful part of the body must be held in check. Faith can do it. Faith acts wisely. It gives us the ability to choose wisdom that is heavenly and shun wisdom that is earthly. Faith produces separation from the world and submission to God. It provides us with the ability to resist the Devil and humbly draw near to God. Finally, faith waits patiently for the coming of the Lord. Through trouble and trial it stifles complaining.

The name Iakobos (James) in 1:1 is the basis for the early title Iakobu Epistole, "Epistle of James." Iakobos is the Greek form of the Hebrew name Jacob, a Jewish name common in the first century.

Date: _______________Day 67

Daily Reading. Chapters: Job 36 – 42;
Ps.41 – 43; Prov.13 – 15; James 1- 5;

Daily Devotion. Write scriptures from your daily reading – Day 67.

Make the scriptures you used personal.
How did your daily scriptures minister to you?

Date: _______________Day 68

Daily Reading. Chapters: Eccl.1- 6;
Ps.44 – 46; Prov.16 – 18; 1Pet.1 – 5;

Daily Devotion. Write scriptures from your daily reading – Day 68.

Make the scriptures you used personal.
How did your daily scriptures minister to you?

Date: _______________Day 69

Daily Reading. Chapters: Eccl.7 – 12;
Ps.47 – 50; Prov.19 – 21; 2Pet.1- 3;

Daily Devotion. Write scriptures from your daily reading - Day 69.

Make the scriptures you used personal.
How did your daily scriptures minister to you?

Date: _______________Day 70

Daily Reading. Chapters: Song 1 – 8;
Ps.51 – 54; Prov.22 – 24; 1John 1 – 5; 2John

Daily Devotion. Write scriptures from your daily reading – Day 70.

Make the scriptures you used personal.
How did your daily scriptures minister to you?

Psalms

Outlines

Book I. The Genesis Book Prayer of Faith in
Adversity 1 - 41

Exceptions: Praise Psalm, 8, 24, 29 and 33
Royal Praise 2, 21
Psalms of Righteousness, 1 and 15
Penitential, 32
Revelation, 19

Book II. Exodus Book Prayers of
Faith in Adversity 42 - 72

Exceptions: Praise Psalms, 47, 48, 50, 65 - 68
Penitential 51
Imprecation 58 and 59

Book III. Leviticus Book of Trust 73 - 89

Exceptions: Praise Psalms, 78 and 81
Historical, 105 and 106
Love for Zion, 84 and 87
Rebuke the Wicked

Book IV. Numbers Book Psalms
Praise 90 - 106

Exceptions: Faith in Adversity, 90, 91 and 102
Historical, 105 and 106
Psalm of Righteousness 101

Book V. Deuteronomy Book Psalms of praises, Trust in Trouble 107 - 150

Exception: Royal Psalms, 110 and 132
National Distress 129 and 137
Psalms of Righteousness 112 and 116
Revelations 119
Love for Zion 122
Songs of Degrees, 120 - 134
Hallel Psalms praise, 113 - 118, 136, 146 - 150

The Book of PSALMS

The Book of Psalms is the largest and perhaps most widely used book in the Bible. It explores the full range of human experience in a very personal and practical way. Its 150 "songs" run from the Creation through the patriarchal, theocratic, monarchic, exilic, and postexilic periods. The tremendous breath of subject matter in the Psalms includes diverse topics, such as jubilation, war, peace, worship, judgment, messianic prophecy, praise and lament. The Psalms were set to the accompaniment of stringed instruments and served as the temple hymnbook and devotional guide for the Jewish people.

The Book of Psalms was gradually collected and originally unnamed, perhaps due to the great variety of material. It came to be known as Sepher Tehillim-"Book of Praises" because almost every psalm contains some note of praise to God. The Septuagint uses the Greek word Psalmoi as its title for this book, meaning "Poems Sung to the Accompaniment of Musical Instruments." It also calls it the term Psalter. The Latin title is Liber Psalmorum, "Book of Psalms."

Proverbs

Outline	Chapters and Verses
Title and Prologue	1: 1 – 7
Fourteen Words of Exhortation	
Wealth by violence And Wisdom's	1:8 – 33
Wisdom from God to discern Good and Evil Ways	2: 1 – 22
God Honors Those Who Honor Him	3: 1 – 10
Discipline Precious beyond Riches	3: 11 – 20
Loving Your Neighbor	3: 21 – 35
Wisdom is a Family Treasure	4: 1 – 9
Wisdom	4: 10 – 19
Right Purpose and Worthy Conduct	4: 20 – 27
Beware of Lust	5: 1 – 6
Love versus Lust	5: 7 – 23
Idleness and Deceit	6: 1 – 19
Folly of Adultery	6: 20 – 35
Parable on Chastity	7: 1 – 27
Wisdom Portrayed	8: 1 – 9: 18
Solomon' s Proverbs and Word Of Wisdom	10:1 – 29:27
Word of Wisdom Wise Men	22:17 – 24:34
Hezekiah Copied Solomon' s	25:1 – 29:27
The Words of Agur	30:1 – 33
The Words of Lemuel	31:1 – 9

The Book of PROVERBS

The key word is Proverbs is wisdom, "the ability to live life skillfully." A godly life in an ungodly world, however, is no simple assignment. Proverbs provides God's detailed instructions, for His people to deal successfully with the practical affairs of everyday life: how to relate to God, parents, children, neighbors, and government. Solomon, the principal author, uses a combination of poetry, parables, parables, pithy questions, short stories, and wise maxims to give in strikingly memorable form the common sense and divine perspective necessary to handle life's issues.

Because Solomon, the pinnacle of Israel's wise men, was the principal contributor, the Hebrew title of this book is Mishle Shelomoh, "Proverbs of Solomon" (1:1). The Greek title is Paroimiai Salomintos, "Proverbs pf the words pro "for" and verba "words" to describe the way the proverbs concentrate many words into few. The rabbinical writings called Proverbs Sepher Hokhmah, "Book of Wisdom."

The Book of ECCLESIASTES

The key word is Ecclesiates is vanity, "the futile emptiness of trying to be happy apart from God." The Preacher (traditionally taken to be Solomon - 1:1, 12-the wisest, richest influential king in Israel's history) looks at life "under the sun" (1:9) and, from the human perspective, declares it all to be empty. Power, popularity, prestige, pleasure-nothing can fill the God-shaped void in man's life but God Himself! But once seen from God's perpective, like takes on meaning and purpose, causing Solomon to exclaim, "Eat, drink, rejoice, do good, live joyfully, fear God, and keep His commandments. Skepticism and despair melt away when life is viewed as a daily gift from God.

The Hebrew title Qoheleth is a rare phrase, found only in Eclesiastes (1:1, 2, 12; 7:27; 12:8-10). It comes from the word quhal, "to convoke an assembly, to assemble." Thus, it mean "One Who Addresses an Assembly," "A Preacher."

The Septuagint used the Greek word Ekklesiastes as its title for this book. Derived from yhe word ekklesia, "assembly," "congregation," "church," it simply means "Preacher." The Latin Ecclesiates means "Speaker before an Assembly."

Ecclesiastes

Outline	Chapters and Verses
All is Vanity	1: 1, 2
The Weary Round	
Of Nature	1: 3 – 11
Of Experience	1: 12 – 18
Of Pleasures	2: 1 – 11
One' s Successor may be a Fool	2: 12 – 23
Better Enjoy One's Work	2: 24 – 26
Time and Eternity	3: 1 – 22
Political Economy	4: 1 – 16
Religion and Life	5: 1 – 6: 12
Wise Words	7: 1 – 29
Kings and the King	8: 1 – 17
The Last Enemy	9: 1 – 16
More Wise Words	9: 17 – 11: 7
Old Age	11: 8 – 12: 7
Preacher' s Text	12: 8 – 12
View of Judgment	12: 13 – 14

Song of Solomon

Outline	Chapters and Verses
Book Title	1: 1
The Shulamite and Her Beloved	1: 2 – 2: 7
Love of the Shulamite and Her Beloved	2: 8 – 3: 5
Solemnization of Their Marriage	3: 6 – 5: 1
Temporary Absence Followed by Happy Reunion	5: 2 – 8: 4
Bridegroom and Bride contrary of their Unquenchable Love	8: 5 – 14

The SONG Of SOLOMON

The Song of Solomon is a love song written by Solomon and abounding in metaphors and oriental imagery. Historically, it depicts the wooing and wedding of a shepherdess by King Solomon, and the joys and heartaches of wedded love.

Allegorically, it pictures Israel as God's betrothed bride (Hos.2: 19, 20), and the church as the bride of Christ. As human life finds it's highest fulfillment in the love of man and woman, as spiritual life finds it's highest fulfillment in the love of God for His people and Christ for His church.

The book reads like scenes in a dream with three main speakers: the bride (Shulamite woman), the king (Solomon), and a chorus (daughters of Jerusalem).

The Hebrew title Shir Hashirim comes from 1:1, "The song of songs." The Greek title Asma Asmaton and the Latin Canticorum also means "Song of Songs" or "The Best Song." The name Canticles ("ongs") is derived from the Latin title. Because Solomon is mentioned in 1:1, the book ias also known as the Song of Solomon.

Date: _______________Day 71

Daily Reading. Chapters: Isa.1 – 7;
Ps.55 – 58; Prov.25 – 27; 3 John Jude

Daily Devotion. Write scriptures from your daily reading – Day 71.

Make the scriptures you used personal.
How did your daily scriptures minister to you?

Date: ________________Day 72

Daily Reading. Chapters: Isa.8 – 14;
Ps.59 – 62; Prov.28 – 31; Rev.1 – 2;

Daily Devotion. Write scriptures from your daily reading – Day 72.

Make the scriptures you used personal.
How did your daily scriptures minister to you?

Date: ________________Day 73

Daily Reading. Chapters: Isa.15 – 21;
Ps.63 – 65; Prov.1 – 3; Rev.3

Daily Devotion. Write scriptures from your daily reading – Day 73.

Make the scriptures you used personal.
How did your daily scriptures minister to you?

1 Peter

Outline	Chapters and Verses
Peter Greet His Readers	1: 1 – 2
The Trinitarian Doxology	1: 3 – 12
Our Relation to God	1: 13 – 2: 10
Be Holy in all Your Behavior	
Behavior Yourselves with Fear	
Ransomed by the Blood of Jesus	
Love One Another	
Come to the Living Stone	
Built into a Spiritual House	
You are a Chosen People	
Our Relation to Men	2: 11 – 3: 12
Be Subject to Human Institution	
Servants, be Submissive to Your Masters	
Wives, be Submissive to Your Husband	
Husband, Live Selflessly with Your Wives	
Unity of Spirit	
Blessing for Righteousness' Sake	3: 13 – 5: 11
When You Suffer for Wrong	
Baptism is a Sign of Our Death to Sin	
The End is at Hand, Walk in Unfailing Love	
Salutation	5: 12 – 14

The First Epistle of PETER

Persecution can cause either growth or bitterness in the Christian life. Response determines the result. In writing to Jewish believers struggling in the midst of persecution, Peter encourages them to conduct themselves courageously for the Person and program of Christ. Both their character and conduct must be above reproach. Having been born again to a living hope, they are to imitate the Holy One who has called them. The fruit of that character will be conduct rooted in submission: citizens to government, servants to masters, wives to husbands, husbands to wives, and Christian to one another.

Only after submission is fully understood; does Peter deal with the difficult are of suffering. The Christians are not to think it "strange concerning the fiery trial which is to try you, as though some strange thing happened unto you" (4:12), but are tom rejoice as partakers of the suffering of Christ. That response to life is truly the climax of one's submission to the good hand of God.

The epistle begins with the phrase Petro apostolos Iesou Christou, "Peter, an apostle of Jesus Christ." This is the basis of the early title Petrou A, the "First of Peter."

The Second Epistle of PETER

First Peter deals with problems from the outside; Second Peter deals with problems from the inside. Peter writes to warn the believers about the false teachers who are peddling damaging doctrine. He begins by urging them to keep close watch on their personal lives. The Christian life demands diligence in pursuing moral excellence, knowledge, self-control, perseverance, godliness, brotherly kindness, and selfless love.

By contrast, the false teachers are sensual, arrogant, greedy and covetous. They scoff at the thought of future judgment and live their lives if the present would be the pattern for the future. Peter reminds them that although God may be long suffering in sending judgment, ultimately it will come. In view of the fact, believers should live lives of godliness, freedom from guilt, and steadfastness.

The statement of authorship in 1:1 is very clear: "Simon Peter, a servant and an apostle of Jesus Christ." To distinguish this epistle from the first by Peter it was given the Greek title Petrou, B, the "Second of Peter."

2 Peter

Outline	Chapters and Verses
Peter Greet His Readers	1: 1 – 2
Knowledge of the World	1: 3 – 21
Become Come Partakers Of the Divine Nature	
Remember God's Word	
The Prophetic Word Made Sure	
False Teachers	2: 1 – 22
The Coming of the Lord	3: 1 – 18
Scoffers Question the Lord's Coming	
Destroy by Fire	
Hasten the Lord's Coming	

Isaiah

Outline	Chapters and Verses
Volume of Rebuke and Promise	1: 1 – 6: 13
Volume of Immanuel	7: 1 – 12: 6
God's Judgment	13: 1 – 23:6
Volume of General Judgment And Promise	24: 1 – 27: 13
Volume of Woes Upon the Unbelievers of Israel	28: 1 – 29
Second Volume of General Judgment and Promise	
Volume of Hezekiah	36: 1 – 36: 8
Volume of Comfort	40: 1 – 66: 24
The Purpose of Peace	
The Prince of Peace	
The Program of Peace	

The Book of ISAIAH

ISAIAH is like a miniature Bible. The first thirty-nine chapters (like the thirty-nine books of the Old Testament_ are filled with judgment upon immoral and idolatrous men. Judah has sinned; the surrounding nations have sinned; the whole earth has sinned. Judgment must come, for God cannot allow such blatant sin to go unpunished forever. But the final twenty-seven chapters (like the twenty-seven books of the New Testament) declare a message of hope. The Messiah is coming as a Savior and a Sovereign to bear a cross and wear a crown.

Isaiah's prophetic ministry, spanning the reigns of four kings of Judah, covers at least forty years.

Yesha 'yahu and its shortened form Yeshaiah mean "Yahweh Is Salvation." This name is an excellent summary of the contents of the book. The Greek form in the Septuagint is Hesaias, and the Latin form is Esaias or Isaias.

The First Epistle of JOHN

GOD is light; God is love; and God is life is enjoying a Delightful fellowship with that God of light, love and life, and he desperately desires that his spiritual children enjoy the same fellowship.

God is light. Therefore, to engage in fellowship with Him we walk in light and not in darkness. As we walk in the light, we will regularly confess our sins, allowing the blood of Christ to continually us. Two major roadblocks to hinder this walk will be falling in love with the world and falling for the alluring lies of false teachers.

God is love. Since we are His children we must walk in love. In fact, John says that if we do not love, we do not know God. Love is more than just words; it is actions. Love is giving, not getting. Biblical love is unconditional in its nature. Christ's love fulfilled those qualities and when that brand of love characterizes us, we will be free of self-condemnation and experience confidence before God.

God is life. Those who fellowship with Him must possess His quality of life. Spiritual life begins with spiritual birth which occurs through faith in Jesus Christ. Faith in Jesus Christ infuses us with God's life-eternal life.

Although the apostle John's name is not found in this book, it was given the title Ioannou A, the "First of John."

The Second Epistle of JOHN

"Let him thinketh he standeth he standeth take heed lest he fall" (1Cor. 10:12). These words of the apostle Paul could well stand as a subtitle for John's little epistle. The recipients, a chosen lady and her children, were obviously standing. They were walking in truth, remaining faithful to the commandments they had received from the Father. John in deeply pleased to be able to commend them.

But he takes nothing for granted. Realizing that standing is just one step removed from falling, he hesitates not at all to issue a reminder: "love one another" (v.5). The apostle admits that this is not new revelation, but hr views it sufficiently important to repeat. Loving one another, he stresses, is equivalent to walking according to God's commandments.

John indicates, however, that this must be discerning. It is not a naïve, unthinking, open to anything and anyone kind of love. Biblical love is a matter of choice; it is dangerous and foolish to float through life with impetuous love. False teachers abound who do not acknowledge Christ as having come in the flesh. It is false charity to open the door to false teaching. We must have fellowship with God. We must have fellowship with Christians. But we must not have fellowship with false teachers.

The "elder" of verse 1 has been traditionally identified with the apostle John, resulting in the Greek title Ioannou B, the Second of John."

1, 2, 3 John and Jude

Outline	Chapters and Verses
1 John	
The Basis of Christian Life	1: 1 – 5
What it Mean to walk in the Light	1: 6 – 2: 2
Fellowship with the Father	2: 3 – 28
Righteousness, the Mark of Sonship	2: 29 – 3: 24
Practice of Spiritual Discrimination	4: 1 – 6
Love, the Proof of Sonship	4: 7 – 21
Great Assurances of the Christian	5: 1 – 21
Second John	
Walk in Truth and Love	vv. 1- 6
Unscriptural Ways Contrasted	vv. 7- 9
Conclusion	vv. 12 –13
Third John	
Greeting to Gaius and Commendations	vv. 1 – 8
Leaders Contrasted	vv. 9 – 12
Conclusion	vv. 13 – 14
Jude	
Greeting and Purpose	vv.1 – 4
God's Past Judgment Upon Evil People	vv. 5 – 11
Indictment of the false Christian	vv. 17 – 23
Doxology	vv. 17 – 23

The Third Epistle of John

In Third John the apostle encouraged fellowship with Christian brothers. Following his expression of love for Gaius, John assures him of his prayers for his health and voices his joy over Gaius's persistent walk in truth and for the manner in which in he shows hospitality and support for missionaries who have come to his church.

But not everyone in the church feels the same way. Diotrephes' heart is one hundred and eighty degrees removed from Gaius's heart. He is no longer living in love. Pride has taken precedence in his life. He has refused John written for the church, fearing; that his authority might be superseded by that of the apostle. He also has accused John of evil words and refused to eccept missionaries. He forbids other to do so and even expels them from the church if they disobey him. John uses this negative example as an opportunity to encourage Gaius to continue his hospitality. Demrtrius has a good testmony and may even be one of those turned away by Diotrephes. He is widely known for his good character and his loyalty to the truth. Here he is well commended by John and stands as a positive example for Gaius.

The Greek title of First, Second and Third John is Ioannou A, B and G. The G is gamma, the third letter of Greek alphabet; Ioannou G means the "Third of John."

The Epistle of JUDE

FIGHT! Contend! Do battle! When apostasy arises, when false teachers emerge, when the truth of God is attacked, it is time; to fight for the faith. Only believers who are spiritual "in shape" can answer the summons. At the beginning of his letter Jude focuses on the believers' common salvation, but feeling compelled to challenge them to content for the faith. The danger is real. False teachers have crept into the church turning God's grace into unbounded license to do as they please. Jude reminds such men of God's past dealing with unbelieving Israel, disobedient angels, and wicked Sodom and guard. The challenge is great, but so is the God who is able to keep them from stumbling.

The Greek title Iouda, "Of Jude," comes from the name Ioudas appears in verse 1. This name, which can be translated

Jude or Judas, was popular in the first century because of Judas Maccabaeus (died 160 B.), a leader of the Jewish resistance against Syria during the Maccabean revolt.

Date: ________________Day 74

Daily Reading. Chapters: Isa.22 – 28;
Ps.66 – 63; Prov.4 – 6; Rev.4;

Daily Devotion. Write scriptures from your daily reading – Day 74.

Make the scriptures you used personal.
How did your daily scriptures minister to you?

Date: ________________Day 75

Daily Reading. Chapters: Isa.29 – 35;
Ps.69 – 77; Prov.7 – 9; Rev.5;

Daily Devotion. Write scriptures from your daily reading – Day 75.

Make the scriptures you used personal.
How did your daily scriptures minister to you?

Revelation

Outline	Chapters and Verses
Introduction	1: 1 – 8
Vision of the Risen Christ	1: 9 – 20
Letter to the Seven Churches	2: 1 – 3: 22
The Seven Seals Opened	6:1 – 17; 81- 5
The Seven Trumpets Blow	8:6 – 9;11:15 – 19
The Women and the Dragon	12: 1 – 17
The Two Beasts	13: 1 – 18
The 144,000 on Mt. Zion	14: 6 – 20
The Seven Vials of Wrath	5: 1 – 16: 21
The Great Harlot: Babylon	17: 1 – 18
The Great City: Babylon	18: 1 – 24
Jesus Return in Power	19: 11 – 21
Satan Bound and the Milennial Kingdom	20: 1 – 6

The Final Revelation	20: 7 – 10
Great White Throne Judgment	20: 11 – 15
The New Heavens and Earth	21: 1 – 8
The New Jerusalem	21:9 – 22:5
Epilogue	22: 6 – 21

THE REVELATION OF JESUS CHRIST

Just as Genesis is the book of beginnings, Revelation is the book of consummation. In, the divine program of redemption is brought to fruition, and the holy name of God is vindicated before all creation. Although there are numerous prophecies in the Gospels and Epistles; Revelation is the book in the New Testament book that focuses primarily on prophetic events. Its title means "unveiling" or "disclosure." Thus, the book is an unveiling of the character and program of God. Penned by John during his exile on the island of Patmos, Revelation centers around vision and symbols of the resurrected Christ, who alone has authority to judge the earth, to remark it, and to rule it in righteousness.

The title of this book in Greek text is Apokalysis Ioannou,

Revelation of John." It is also known as the Apocalypse, a transliteration of the word apokalypsis, meaning "unveriling," "disclosure," or "revelation." Thus, theword is an unveiling of that which otherwise could not be known. A better title comes from the first verse: Apokalypsis Iesou Christou, "Revelation of Jesus Christ." This could be taken as a revelation; which came from Christ or a revelation which is about Christ – both are appropriate. Because of the unified contents of the book, it should not be called Revelations.

Jeremiah

Outline	Chapters and Verses
Jeremiah, God's Warrior	
Jeremiah Call and Commission	11 - 13:1 - 27
Judah's Situation: Sickness, Folly, Blindness, Treachery, Idolatry, Faithlessness And Rebellion	
Jeremiah's Encounter	14:1 - 25:38
Conflict of Faith	26:1 - 29:32
The Substance of Faith	30:1 - 31:40
The Action of Faith	32:1 - 44
The Vision of Faith	33:1 - 26
Jeremiah, God's Watchman	34:1 - 45:5
Jeremiah, God's Witness to the Nation	46:1 - 52:34

The Book of JEREMIAH

The Book of Jeremiah is the prophecy of a man divinely called in his youth from the priest-city of Anathoth. A heartbroken prophet with a heartbreaking message, Jeremiah labors far more than forty years proclaiming a message of doom to the stiff-necked people of Judah. Despised and persecuted by his countrymen, Jeremiah bathes his harsh prophecies in tears of compassion. His broken heart causes him to write a broken book, which is difficult to arrange chronologically or topically. But through his sermons and signs he faithfully declares that surrender to God's will is the only way to escape calamity.

Yirmeyahu or Yirmeyah literally means "Yahweh Throws," perhaps in the sense of laying a foundation. It may effectively mean "Yahweh Establishes, Appoints, or Sends." The Greek form of the Hebrew name in the Septuagint is Hieremia, and the Latin form is Jeremias.

Lamentation

Outline	Chapters and Verses
The Meaning of Jerusalem's Afflictions	
Description of Jerusalem's Afflictions	1: 1 - 7
Explanation of Jerusalem's Afflictions	1: 8 - 18
Effect of Jerusalem's Afflictions	1: 19 - 22
The Reality of Jerusalem' s Afflictions	
Adversary	2: 1 - 8
Agony	2: 9 - 16
Entreaty	2: 17 - 22
Factors in Jerusalem's Afflictions	
The Rod of God's Wrath	3: 1 - 20
The Multitude of God's Mercies	3: 21 - 39
The Justice of God's Judgment	3: 40 - 54
The Prayer of Gods People	3: 55 - 66
Lessons from Jerusalem's Afflictions	
Vanity of Human Glory	4: 1 - 12
Vanity of Human Leadership	4: 13 - 16
Vanity of Human Resources	4: 17 - 20
Vanity of Human Pride	4: 21 - 22
The Issues of Jerusalem's Afflictions	
Invokes God's Grace	5: 1 - 18
Invokes God's Glory	5: 19 - 22

THE BOOK of LAMENTATIONS

Lamentations describes the funeral of the city. It is a tearstained portrait of the once proud Jerusalem, now reduced to rubble by the invading Babylonian hordes. In a five-poem dirge, Jeremiah exposes his emotions. A death has occurred; Jerusalem lies barren.

Jeremiah writes his lament in acrostic or alphabetical fashion. Beginning each chapter with the first letter A (aleph) he progresses verse by verse through the Hebrew alphabet, literally weeping from A to Z. And then, in the midst of this terrible holocaust, Jeremiah triumphantly cries out, "Great is thy faithfulness" (3:23). In the face of death and destruction, with life seemingly failed him in the past. God he knows and loves, Jeremiah finds hope and comfort.

The Hebrew title of this Book comes from the first word of chapters 1, 2, and 4: Ekah, "Ah, how!" Another Hebrew word Ginoth ("Elegies" or "Lamentations") has also been used as the title because it better represents the word contents of the book. The Greek title Threnoi means "Dirges" or Laments," and the Latin title Threni ("Tears" or Lamentations") was derived from this word. The subtitle in Jerome's Vulgate reads: "Id est lamentationes Jeremiae prophetae" and this became the basis for the English title "The Lamentations of Jeremiah."

Date: ________________Day 76

Daily Reading. Chapters: Isa.36 – 42;
Ps.78 – 82; Prov.10 – 12; Rev.6;

Daily Devotion. Write scriptures from your daily reading – Day 76.

Make the scriptures you used personal.
How did your daily scriptures minister to you?

Date: _______________Day 77

Daily Reading. Chapters: Isa.43 – 50; Ps.83 – 86; Prov.13 – 15; Rev.7;

Daily Devotion. Write scriptures from your daily reading – Day 77.

Make the scriptures you used personal.
How did your daily scriptures minister to you?

I will sing of the mercies of the Lord forever:
With my mouth will I make known thy faithfulness
to all generations.

Find and Write the Verse ____________________________.

Ezekiel

Outline	Chapters and Verses
Israel, A Rebellious People	1: 1 – 3: 24: 27
God's sends Ezekiel	
Vision of Israel Doom	
New of the fall of the Rebellious House	
Foreign Nations, Guilty of Crimes against And People, will be Destroyed	25:1 – 32: 32
Chastened Israel will be Restored	33: 1 – 39: 29
News of the fall of Jerusalem	
The Promise of Restoration	
Under an Eternal King	
Hills of Israel	
Heart of Flesh	
Life	
Unity	
Safety from Evil	
The Vision of Restoration	40: 1 48: 35
Temple of a Restored People	
The Glory of the Lord Enters the Temple	
Worship of the Restored People	
Living Waters and the Promised Land of Inheritance	

The Book of EZEKIEL

Enekiel, a priest and a prophet, ministers during the darkest days of Judah's history" the seventy-year period of Babylonian captivity. Carried to Babylon before the final assault on Jerusalem, Ezekiel uses prophecies, parables, signs, and symbols to dramatize God's message to His exiled people.

Through hey are like dry bones in the sun. G0od will reassemble them and breathe life into the nation one again. Present judgment will be followed by future glory so that "ye shall know that I am the LORD" (6:7).

The Hebrew name Yehezke'l means "God Strenghtens" or "Strengthened by God." Ezekiel is indeed strengthened by God for the prophetic ministry to which he is called (3:8, 9). The name occurs twice in the book and nowhere else in the Old Testament. The Greek form in the Septuagint is Iezekiel and the Latin form in the Vulgate is Ezechiel.

The Book of DANIEL

Daniel's life and ministry bridge the entire seventy-year period of Babylonian captivity. Deported to become God's prophetic mouthpiece to the government service, Daniel becomes God's prophetic mouthpiece to the gentile and Jewish world declaring God's present and eternal purpose. Nine of the twelve chapters is his book revolve around dreams, including God-given visions involving trees, animals, beasts and images. In both his personal adventures and prophetic visions, Daniel shows God's guidance, intervention, and power in the affairs of men.

The name Daniye'l or Dani'el means "God Is My Judge," and the book is, of course, named after the author and principal character. The Greek form Daniel is Septuagint is the basis for the Latin and English titles.

Daniel

Outline	Chapters and Verses
Miscellaneous Babylon Experiences Captivity and Preparation for Count Service	1: 1 - 21
Nebuchadrezzar's Fourfold Image	2: 1 – 49
The Image of Gold: The Fiery Furnace	3: 1 – 30
Dream of the Tree: Interpretation	4: 1 – 37
The Hand Writing on the Wall	5: 1 – 31
Darius, Daniel and the Lion's Den	6: 1 – 28
Vision of Four Empire and a Fifth	
Daniel's Four - Beast Vision: The Ancient of Days	7: 1 – 28
Daniel's Ram: He Goat and Little Horn Vision	8: 1 – 27
The Vision for Daniel's People and City	
Confession, Intercession, and Prayer For Restoration	9: 1 – 19
The Prophecy of the Seventy "Week"	9: 20 – 27
Daniel's Vision of the Glory of God	10: 1 – 19
Prophecies Concerning Persia, Greece and Antiochus	10:20 – 11: 35
The King at the End	1: 36 – 45
Michael and the Resurrection	12: 1 – 3
Events to the End	12: 4 – 13

The Book of HOSEA

Hosea, whose name means "Salvation," ministers to the northern kingdom of Israel (also called Ephraim, after its largest tribe). Outwardly, the nation is enjoying a time of prosperity and growth; but inwardly, moral corruption and spiritual adultery permeate the people. Hosea, instructed by God to marry a women name Gomer, finds his domestic life to be an accurate and tragic dramatization of the unfaithfulness of God's people. During his half century of prophetic ministry, Hosea repeatedly echoes his threefold message: God abhors the sins of His people; judgment is certain; but God's loyal love stands firm.

The names Hosea, Joshua, and Jesus are all derived from the same Hebrew root word. The word hoshea means "salvation," but "Joshua" and "Jesus" include an additional idea: "Yahweh Is Salvation." As God's messenger, Hosea offers the possibility of salvation if only the nation will turn from idolatry back to God.

Israel's last king, Hoshea, has the same as the prophet even though the English Bible spells them differently. Hosea in the Greek and Latin is Osee.

The Book of JOEL

Disater strikes the southern kingdom of Judah without warning. An ominous black cloud desends upon the land-the dreaded locusts. In a spokesman during the reign of Joash (835-796 B.C), seizes this occasion to proclaim God's message. Although the locust plague has been a terrible judgment for sin, God's future judgment during the day of the Lord will make plague pale by comparison. In that day, God will destroy His enemies, but bring unparalleled blessing to those who faithfully obey Him.

The Hebrew name Yo'el means "YahwehIs God." This name is appropriate to the theme of the book, which emphasizes God's sovereign work in history. The courses of nature and nations are in His hand. The Greek equivalent is Ioel, and the Latin is Joel.

The Book of AMOS

Amos prophesies, during a period of national optimism is Israel. Business is booming and boundaries are bulging. But below the surface, greed and injustice are festering. Hypocritical religious motions have replaced true worship creating a false sense of security and growing callousness to God's disciplining hand. Famine, drought, plagues, death, destruction-nothing can force the people to their knees.

Amos, the farmer-turned-prophet, lashes out at sin unflinchingly, trying to visualize the nearness of God's judgment and mobilize the nation to repentance. The nation; like a basket of rotting fruit, stand ripe for judgment because of its hypocrisy and spiritual indifference.

The name Amos is derived from the Hebrew root amas, "to lift a burden, to carry." Thus, his name means "Burden" or Burden-Bearer." Amos lives up to the meaning of his name by bearing his divinely given burden of declaring judgment to rebllious Israel. The Greek and Latin title are both transliterated in English as Amos.

Hosea, Joel, and Amos

Outline	Chapters and Verses

Hosea

Hosea's Heartbreaking Home Life Caused By Gomer's Infidelity, Illustrates Israel's Unfaithful to God	1: 1 3:5
The Nation Israel Unrepentant, Is Challenged by the Preacher to Come Home to the Faithful God	4:1 - 14:9

Joel

The Lord Plague and its Removal	1: 1 - 2:27
The Future Day of the Lord	2: 28 - 3: 21

Amos

Prophecies Against the Nations	1: 1 - 2: 16
Three Discourses Against Israel	3: 1 - 6:14
Five Symbolical Visions of Israel's Condition	7: 1 - 9: 10

Date: _______________Day 78

Daily Reading. Chapters: Isa.51 – 58;
Dan.1 – 6 Ps.87 – 88; Prov.16; Rev.8

Daily Devotion. Write scriptures from your daily reading – Day 78.

Make the scriptures you used personal.
How did your daily scriptures minister to you?

Date: _______________Day 79

Daily Reading. Chapters: Isa.59 – 66;
Dan.7 – 12; Ps.89; Prov.17; Rev.9;

Daily Devotion. Write scriptures from your daily reading – Day 79.

Make the scriptures you used personal.
How did your daily scriptures minister to you?

Date: ________________Day 80

Daily Reading. Chapters: Jer.1 – 7; Ezek.1- 5
Hos.1 – 7; Ps.90; Rev.10;

Daily Devotion. Write scriptures from your daily reading – Day 81.

Make the scriptures you used personal.
How did your daily scriptures minister to you?

Obadiah and Jonah

Outline	Chapters and Verses

Obadiah

An Oracle of the Lord against Edom	vv. 1 – 4
The Awful Manifestation	vv. 5 – 9
Esau's Sin Against His Brother Jacob	vv. 10 – 14
The Wider Context: The Day Of the Lord	vv.15 – 18
House of Jacob to "Possess Their Possessions"	vv.19 – 21

Jonah

The Rebellious Prophet	1: 1 – 17
The Lord calls: Jonah Rebels	
The Lord Interposes a Storm	
The Sailors Intervene	
The Lord Send a Big Fish	
The Reinstated Prophet	2: 1 – 3: 10
Jonah Prays	
The Lord Delivers Jonah	
Jonah Obeys the Call	
King and Ninevites Repent	
The Lord withhold Judgment	
The Retired Prophet	4: 1 – 11
The Lord Displeases Jonah	
Worm and the Gourd	
Jonah Displeases the Lord	
God' Reply	

The Book of OBADIAH

A struggle that began in the womb between twin brothers, Esau and Jacob, eventuates in a struggle between their respective descendants, the Edomites and Israelites. For the Edomites' stubborn refusal to aid Israel, first during the time of wilderness wandering (Num.20: 14 - 21) and later during a time of invasion, they are roundly condemned by Obadiah. This little-known prophet describes their crimes, tries their case, and pronounces their judgment: total destruction.

The Hebrew name Obadyah means "Worshiper of Yahweh" or "Servant of Yahweh." The Greek title in the Septuagint is Odabiou, and the Latin title is the Vulgate is Abdias.

The Book of JONAH

Nineveh is northeast; Tarshish is west. When God calls Jonah to preach repentance to the wicked Ninevites, the prophet knows that God's mercy may follow. He turns down the assignment and heads for Tarshish instead. But once God has dampened his spirit (by tossing him of the boat and into the water) and into the fish), Jonah realizes God is serious about His command.

Nineveh must hear the word of the Lord; therefore Jonah goes. Although the preaching is a success, the preacher comes away angry and discouraged and he must learn firsthand of God's compassion for sinful men.

Yonah is the Hebrew word for "dove." The Septuagint hellenized this word into Ionas, and Latin Vulgate used the title Jonas.

Date: _______________Day 81

Daily Reading. Chapters: Jer.8 – 14; Ezek.6 -10
Hos.8 – 14; Ps.91; Prov.19; Rev.11;

Daily Devotion. Write scriptures from your daily reading – Day 81.

___

___

___

___

___

___

___

___

___

___

___

Make the scriptures you used personal.
How did your daily scriptures minister to you?

___

___

___

___

___

___

___

___

___

___

___

___

___

___

___

___

___

___

___

___

Date: ______________Day 82

Daily Reading. Chapters: Jer.15 – 21; Ezek.11 - 15
Joel 1 – 3; Ps.92 – 94; Prov.20 – 21; Rev.12

Daily Devotion. Write scriptures from your daily reading – Day 82.

Make the scriptures you used personal.
How did your daily scriptures minister to you?

Micah and Nahum

Outline	Chapter and Verses
Micah	
Identification	1: 1
The Reproof of Samaria and Judah	1: 2 - 3: 12
Appearance of the Lord in Judgment	
The Lord's Denunciation of the	
Rulers, False Prophets, and Priests	
The Comforting Hope of a Redemptive Future	4: 1 - 5: 15
The Lord's Lawsuit with Israel	6: 1 - 16

Nahum

The Prelude	
Introduction	1: 1
The Nature of God	1: 2 - 6
God's Administrated of Justice	1: 7 - 10
Nineveh's Destruction Announced	1:11 -15; 22
As Part of God's Plan	
Nineveh's Destruction to be Complete	2: 1, 3 - 13
Nineveh's Destruction Caused By Sin	3: 1 - 18

The Book of MICAH

Micah, called from his rustic home to be a prophet, leaves his familiar surroundings to deliver a stern message of judgment to the princes and people of Jerusalem. Burdened by the abusive treatment of the poor by the rich and influential, the prophet turns his verbal rebukes upon any who would use their social or political power for personal gain. One-third of Micah's book exposes the sins of his countrymen; another third pictured the punishment God is about to send; and the final third holds out the hope of restoration once that discipline has ended. Through it all, God's righteous demands upon His people are clear: "to do justly, and to love mercy, and to walk humbly with thy God" (6:8).

The name Michayahu ("Who Is Like Yahweh?") is shortened to Michaia. In 7:18, Micah hints at his own name with the phrase "Who is a God like unto thee?" The Greek and Latin titles of this book are Michias and Micha.

The Book of NAHUM

For unto whomsoever much is given, of him shall be much required" (Luke 12:48). Nineveh had been given the privilege of knowing the one true God. Under Jonah's preaching this great gentile city had repented, and Nahum proclaims the downfall of this same city. The Assyrians have forgotten their revival and have returned to their habits of violence, idolatry, and arrogance. As a result, Babylon will so destroy the city that no trace of it will remain - a prophecy fulfilled in painful detail.

The Hebrew word nahum ("comfort," "consolation") is a shortened form of Assyria is a message of comfort and consolation to Judah and all who live in fear of the cruelty of the Assyrians. The title of this book in the Greek and Latin

Bibles is Naoum and Nahum.

Date: _______________Day 83

Daily Reading. Chapters: Jer.22 – 28; Ezek.16 - 19
Amos 1 – 9; Ps.95 – 77; Prov.22 – 25; Rev.13;

Daily Devotion. Write scriptures from your daily
reading - Day 83..

Make the scriptures you used personal.
How did your daily scriptures minister to you?

Date: _______________Day 84

Daily Reading. Chapters: Jer.29 – 36; Ezek.20 – 23
Obadiah Ps.98 – 100; Prov.26 – 31; Rev.14;

Daily Devotion. Write scriptures from your daily reading – Day 84.

Make the scriptures you used personal.
How did your daily scriptures minister to you?

Habakkuk

Outline	Chapters and Verses
Title	1: 1
Problem: God Has Not Judge Moral Depravity Of Judah	1: 2 – 4
God's Solution: The Chaldeans Will Judge Judea	1: 5 – 11
Problem: Why are the wicked Used to Punish the Righteous?	1: 12 – 17

The Book of HABAKKUK

Habakkuk ministers during the "death throes" of the nation of Judah. Although repeatedly called to repentance, the nation stubbornly refuses to change her sinful ways. Habakkuk, knowing the hardheatedness of his countrymen, asks God how long this intolerable condition can continue. God replies that the Babylonians will be His chastening rod upon the nation – an announcement that sends the prophet to his knees. He acknowledges that the just in any generation shall live by faith (2:4), not by sight. Habakkuk concludes by praising God's wisdom even though he does not fully understand God's ways.

Habaqqua is an unusal Hebrew name derive from the verb habaq, "embrace." Thus his name probably means "One Who Embraces" or "Clings." At the end of his book this name becomes appropriate because Habakkuk chooses to cling firmly to God regardless of what happens to his nation (3:16 – 19). The Greek title in the Septuagint is Ambakouk, and the

Latin title in Jerome's Vulgate is Habacuc.

Zephaniah

Outline	Chapters and Verses
Prophecy of God's Judgments	1: 1 – 2: 3
Ancestry and Identity of The Prophet	
Announcement of Certain Judgment	
Announcement of the Day of The Lord	
The Day of Woe	
Judgment is not to be postponed	
Exhortation to Repentance	
God's Judgment of Nations	2: 4 – 3: 8
Promised Blessed	3: 9 – 20
Salvation and Deliverance	
Salvation Demands Praise	

The Book of ZEPHANIAH

During Judah's hectic political and religious history, reform comes from time to time. Zephaniah's forceful prophecy may be factor in the reform that occur during Josiah's reign – a "revival" that produces outward change, but does not fully remove the inward heart of corruption which characterizes the nation. Zephaniah hammers home his message repeatedly that the day of the Lord, Judgment Day, is coming when the malignancy of sin will be dealt with. Israel and her gentile neighbors will soon experience the crushing hand of God's wrath. But after the chastening process is complete, blessing will come in the person of the Messiah, who will be the cause for praise and singing.

Tsephan-yah means "Yahweh Hides" or "Yahweh Has Hidden." Zephaniah was evidently born during the latter part of the reign of King Mansseh. His name may mean that he was "hidden" from Manassesh's atrocities. The Greek and Latin is Sophonias.

Date: ________________Day 85

Daily Reading. Chapters: Jer.37 – 44; Ezek.24 – 28
Jonah 1 – 4; Ps.101; Prov.1 – 3; Rev.15;

Daily Devotion. Write scriptures from your daily reading – Day 85.

Make the scriptures you used personal.
How did your daily scriptures minister to you?

Date: _______________Day 86

Daily Reading. Chapters: Jer.45 – 52; Rev.16; Ezek.27 – 31
Micah 1 – 7; Ps.102 – 104; Prov.4 – 7;

Daily Devotion. Write scriptures from your daily reading – Day86.

Make the scriptures you used personal.
How did your daily scriptures minister to you?

Haggai

Outline	Chapters and Verses
Call to Examination Opening Call to the Rulers General Call to the People	1: 1 – 6
Declaration of Divine Judgment Summons to Build Explanation of Economic Difficulties	1: 7 – 11
Response of the People Movement of Obedience Promise of Divine Help Work Begun	1: 12 – 15
Message of Encouragement Human Disparagement The Divine Presence Glory of the New Home	2: 1 – 9
Promise of Blessing	2: 10 – 19
Confirmation of Zerubbabel	2: 20 – 23

The Book of HAGGAI

With the Babylonian exile in the past, and a newly returned group of Jews back in the land, the work of rebuilding the temple can begin. However sixteen years after the process is begun, the people have yet to finish the project, for their personal affairs have interfered with God's business. Haggai preaches a fiery series of sermons designed to stir up the nation to finish the temple. He calls the builders to renewed courage in the Lord, renewed holiness of life, and renewed faith in God who controls the future.

The etymology and meaning of Haggay is uncertain, but it is probably derived from the Hebrew word hag, "festival," It may also be an abbreviated form of haggiah, "festival of Yahweh." Thur, Haggai's name means "Festal" or Festive," possibly because he was born on the day of a major feast, such as Tabernacle (Haggai's second message takes place during that feast, 2:1). The title in the Septuagint is Aggaios and in the Vulgate it is Aggaeus.

The Book of ZECHARIAH

For a dozen years or more, the task of rebuilding the temple has been half completed, Zechariah is commissioned by God to encourage the people in their unfinished responsibility. Rather than exhorting them to action with strong words of rebuke, Zechariah seeks to encourage them to action by reminding them of the future importance of the temple. The temple must be built, for one day the Messiah's glory will inhabit it. But future blessing is contingent upon present obedience. The people are not merely building a building; they are building the future. With that as their motivation, they can enter into the building project with wholehearted zeal, for their Messiah is coming.

Zekar-yah means "Yahweh Remember" or Yahweh Has Remembered." This theme dominates the whole book: Israel will be blessed because Yahweh remembers the covenant He made with the fathers. The Greek and Latin version of his name is Zacharias.

Zechariah

Outline	Chapters and Verses
Call to Conversion	1: 1 - 6
Visionary Disclosure of God's purposes	1: 7 - 6: 15
Vision One: Appearances Deceive Vision Two: The Destroyers Destroyed Vision Three: Perfect safety of an Open City Vision Four: Satan Silenced Vision Five: The Temple Rebuild By the Spirit Vision Six: The Curse Destroys Sin Vision Seven: Personified Sin Banished From the Land Vision Eight: Four Chariots	
A Prophetic Message to the People	7: 1 - 8: 23
The Emerging Kingdom The King and His Kingdom Two Shepherds Jerusalem Attacked and Delivered Inward Blessing Promised Three fold Purification Death of the Shepherd The Day of the Lord	9: 1 - 14: 21

Date: _______________Day 87

Daily Reading. Chapters: Lam.1- 5; Nah.1 – 3; Ezek.35 – 36
Hab.1 – 3; Ps.105 – 107; Prov.8 – 10; Rev.17;

Daily Devotion. Write scriptures from your daily reading – Day 87.

Make the scriptures you used personal.
How did your daily scriptures minister to you?

Date: _______________Day 88

Daily Reading. Chapters: Ezek.37 - 38; Zep.1 - 3; Hag.1 - 2; Ps.108; Prov.11; Rev. 18;

Daily Devotion. Write scriptures from your daily reading - Day 88.

Make the scriptures you used personal.
How did your daily scriptures minister to you?

The Book of MALACHI

Malachi, a prophet in the days of Nehemiah, directs his message of judgment to a people plagued with corrupt priests, witched practices, and question-and-answer method, Malachi probes deeply into their problems of hypocrisy, infidelity, mixed marriages, divorce, false worship, and arrogance. So sinful has the nation become that God's words to the people no longer have any impact. For four hundred years after Malachi's ringing condemnations, God remains silent. Only with the coming of John the Baptist (prophesied in 3:1) does God again communicate to His people through a prophet's voice. The meaning of the name Mal'aki ("My Messenger") is probably a shortened form of Mal'akya, "Messenger of Yahweh," and it is appropriate to the book which speaks of the coming of the "Messenger of the Covenant" ("messenger" is mentioned three times in 2:7, 3:1). The Septuagint used the title Malachias and also translated it "by the hand of his messenger." The Latin title is Malachi.

Malachi

Outline	Chapters and Verses
Undeniable Love: God's love for Israel	1: 1 – 5
Unacceptable Sacrifices: Corrupt Offering by Corrupt Priest	1: 6 – 14
Unfaithful Obligations: The Priests' Neglect of the Covenant	2: 1 – 9
Unfaithful Husband: Rebuke for Idolatry and Divorce	2: 10 – 10
Unforeseen Judgment: The Coming Of the Unmeasured Blessed:	2: 17 – 3: 6 3: 13 – 4: 3
God's Promise Unnecessary Assertions:	3: 13 – 4: 3
Farewell	4: 4 – 6

Date: _______________Day 89

Daily Reading. Chapters: Ezek.39 - 43; Zech.1 – 8; Ps. 109; Prov.12; Rev.19 - 20;

Daily Devotion. Write scriptures from your daily reading – Day 89.

Make the scriptures you used personal.
How did your daily scriptures minister to you?

Date: ________________Day 90

Daily Reading. Chapters: Ezek. 44– 48; Zech. 9 – 14;
Mal. 1 – 4; Ps. 110; Prov.13; Rev. 21 – 22;

Daily Devotion. Write scriptures from your daily reading – Day 90.

Make the scriptures you used personal.
How did your daily scriptures minister to you?

Need Your Book Published?

Take the Next Step in Faith.

Contact:
Divine Favors Christian Books Publications
1811 Hwy. 138 SW
Riverdale, GA 30295
404.453-0601
www.divinefavors.com

2Corinthians 5: 7

(For We Walk By Faith, And Not By Sight)

To The Readers

I praise and thank God for you.
I pray that God blessed you;
as you fellowship with Him.

Proverbs 1:7

The fear of the Lord is the beginning of knowledge:
But fools despise wisdom and instruction.

John 15: 1 – 5

I AM the true vine, and my Father is the husbandman.

Every branch in Me that beareth not fruit he taketh away:
And every branch that beareth fruit, He purgeth it,
that it may bring forth more fruit.

Now you are clean through the word, which I have spoken unto you.

Abide in me, and I in you. As the branch cannot bear fruit of itself, except it abide in the vine; no more can ye, except ye abide in me.

I am the vine, ye are the branches: He that abideth in me, and I in him, the same bringeth forth much fruit: for without me ye can do nothing

2 Timothy 2:15
Study to shew thyself approved unto God,
a workman that neededth not to be ashamed,
rightly dividing the word of truth.

Jesus said unto her, "I AM the resurrection, And the life: he that believe in me, though he were dead, yet shall he live."

LaVergne, TN USA
17 December 2009

167379LV00001B/201/P

9 781424 313204